TRAVEL SERIES

Bangladesh - A Land of Natural Beauty

Shaykh Mufti Saiful Islām Sāhib's Breath taking & INSPIRATIONAL Journey To Bangladesh

JKN Publications

© Copyright by JKN Publications

First Published in January 2018

ISBN: 978-1-909114-33-3

British Library Cataloguing in Publication Data
A catalogue record for this book is available from the British Library.

All Rights Reserved. No part of this book may be reproduced, stored in a retrieval system or transmitted in any form or by any means, electronic, mechanical, photocopying, recording or otherwise, without the prior permission of the copyright owner.

Publisher's Note:

Every care and attention has been put into the production of this book. If however you find any errors, they are our own, for which we seek Allāh's ﷻ forgiveness and the reader's pardon.

Published by:

JKN Publications
118 Manningham Lane
Bradford
West Yorkshire
BD8 7JF
United Kingdom

t: +44 (0) 1274 308 456 | w: www.jkn.org.uk | e: info@jkn.org.uk

Book Title: Bangladesh– A Land of Natural Beauty

Author: Shaykh Mufti Saiful Islām

Printed by Mega Printing in Turkey

"In the Name of Allāh ﷺ, the Most Beneficent, the Most Merciful"

Contents

Introduction	6
First Visit to Bangladesh	9
Reunion in Bangladesh	11
Tested by Scholars	12
Tarawīh Salāh in Bangladesh	13
Salāh in Jamā'at—An Amazing Incident	13
Political Unrest	15
Second Journey to Bangladesh	16
Amazing Completion of Jalālayn	16
The Journey	17
Arrival in Bangladesh	18
Visit to Two Great Institutes	19
Invitation to All	20
Enquiries into Charity Work	20
Travelling to Various Villages—Akil Pūr	21
Banyachong	21
Modhukhani	22
Satayhāl and Tājpūr	22
Bolorampūr	23
Too Many Invitations	24
Borūna	24
Sunamgonj	25
Mymensingh	26
A Special Wedding	28
Work of Al Kawthar Foundation	28
Third Journey to Bangladesh	30

Contents

My Re-Visit to Bangladesh and the Fatal Accident............. 30
An Unusual Dream... 31
A Second Strange Incident.. 32
Regaining Consciousness.. 33
My Concern for Salāh... 33
A Special Visitor 34
Assessment of Injuries... 35
Transfer from Hospital... 35
Restlessness and Confusion of the People..................... 36
Far-Sightedness of my Beloved Wife............................ 37
Hospitality and Kindness of Shaykh Junaid Al-Habīb......... 37
Arrangements to Return to the UK............................... 38
An Unexpected Phonecall... 39
My Journey Back to the UK....................................... 40
Admission into Hospital... 41
Back Home... 43
Fourth Journey to Bangladesh via Saudi Arabia............. 44
Journey of a Lifetime... 44
Passport Issue... 45
Madīnah Munawwarah.. 47
Makkah Mukarramah.. 52
Prayer for Aleppo... 57
Last Day of Term at JKN Madrasah............................... 59
Bangladesh (Journey According to Dates)...................... 60

Introduction

All praises are due to Allāh ﷻ, —the Magnificent, Lord of all creation. May endless peace and blessings be upon our Beloved Leader and Guide, Muhammad ﷺ, his family, his Companions and those that follow their ways until the Day of Judgement.

In 1971, a land holding a rich history, ruled by people of diverse cultures, religions and creeds was independently named Bangladesh. Bangladesh— a beautiful country with many natural and breath taking sights to visit, has had many leaders of different faiths. In a land where Islām was once an unknown religion, it now has a Muslim population of 146.6 million Muslims.

Islām first entered the Bengali lands during the Khalīfah of Sayyidunā 'Uthmān ؓ through Arabs coming into the country to trade. The Muslim Arab traders brought their culture and faith with them showing Islām through their honest dealings and transactions. Some eventually settled in the land, marrying women from the Bengali land, while the community were assimilating with them.

Islām also reached Bangladesh via political leaders and military rulers such as Ikhtiyār Ad-Dīn Bakhtiyār Khilji, who was the founder of Muslim rule in Bengal in the early 1200's.

In addition to this, Sūfis and Islamic scholars travelled with their companions and preached Islām throughout the country. At this time Islām was a minority religion.

In the 1300's, Bangladesh was being ruled by a tyrant Hindu king who planned to kill all the Muslims. If they sacrificed a cow to eat, they would be brutally killed. The Muslims were being oppressed and they made continuous Du'ā that Islām continues to prevail.

Allāh ﷻ answered the Du'ās of the Muslims and He sent to the land, a scholar that illuminated the country with his noble speech and words of Imān. Hadhrat Shāh-Jalāl Mujarrad Yemeni ﷺ - a simple but respected scholar, who spent his youth in Makkah, travelled to Bangladesh along with 360 people in his Jamā'ah (group).

They entered at a time of corruption and immodesty when people would be walking the streets barely covered. However, they did not rebuke their fellow brothers and sisters by cursing them, rather, they intended to create a new culture in which being modest would be a part of civilisation. Through their peaceful and tranquil teachings, people from all diverse religions of the country flocked in hundreds to attend their circles and gatherings. A large number of Buddhists, Hindus, Sikhs and Animists accepted Islām and instilled its beautiful teachings into their lives.

Over the years, Islām continued and still continues to spread, through the aid of these phenomenal scholars. Many Masājid, Makātib and Madāris were built and the population of Muslims continues to rise.

A Land of Natural Beauty — Introduction

Bangladesh is a beautiful country with many natural and breath taking sights to visit. It is known for its fertile land and hot weather to produce delicious fruits such as large juicy watermelons, jackfruit, leeches, papaya, pomegranates, pineapples, bananas and betel-nut, to name a few.

This book is a compilation of our respected Shaykh's journeys to Bangladesh including visits to famous Madāris and Masājid around the country.

May Allāh ﷻ accept our beloved Shaykh's efforts to spread the Dīn through visiting different countries. May Allāh ﷻ give us the ability to witness and see the beautiful creation of Allāh ﷻ in such countries. Āmīn!

Yumna Ahmad
Student of Jāmiah Khātamun Nabiyeen
(January 2018)

First Visit to Bangladesh

My First Visit Back to my Birthplace in Bangladesh

After moving to the UK at the age of 6, I did not get the opportunity to visit Bangladesh for a very long time. It was only 15 years later, in the year 1996, after I had completed my studies, that my mother expressed to me her yearning to visit Bangladesh. She had also not visited Bangladesh in that interim so she was very keen to reunite with her family after all those years, especially her father as he was unwell at the time.

Hence, we made our preparations and on Wednesday 7th January 1996, myself, my beloved mother and my youngest sister who was 5 years old at the time, travelled to Bangladesh. For the journey, we had organised to travel together from Manchester Airport with my father-in-law and the rest of my in-laws. My wife did not travel with us as my son Naeemul Islām was only two months old at the time.

We commenced our journey at 6:00am from Bradford with our local taxi driver, brother Abdul Khāliq. On the way we stopped for breakfast in Oldham and picked up my in-laws. After reaching the airport, we bid farewell to our well-wishers and relatives, being completely oblivious at that point as to how challenging our journey would turn out to be!

We travelled via Royal Dutch Airlines but due to treacherous weather conditions, the plane could not land at its scheduled destination, Amsterdam Airport and instead, it landed at Rotterdam Airport. From there, we were escorted to Amsterdam Airport via coach so that we could catch our second flight. But it was not destined to be! By the time we reached Amsterdam Airport, the plane had already left.

There was a large number of passengers with us who had also missed the flight and the next flight was not due until after 3 days. After long hours of consultation with the officials, it was decided that we would travel with British Airways instead. However, in order to do that, we would have to travel back to Heathrow Airport in the UK. We had no choice but to accept.

That night, we stayed in one of the hotels of Amsterdam and the following day, we travelled back from Amsterdam to Heathrow Airport via Royal Dutch Airlines. By that time everybody was extremely tired and frustrated.

In the midst of all this chaos, whilst waiting for our flight, my elder brother called me to inform me of the tragic news that my beloved maternal grandfather, Abdul Jabbār had passed away. I was very saddened to learn of his death. I was looking forward to seeing him after so many years but now this would not be possible.

I decided not to break the sorrowful news to my mother at this particular juncture because we were already under so much stress; thus, I intended to tell her at a more appropriate time. However, she could detect from my facial expression that something was not right. I explained to her that grandfather was at rest, there was nothing to worry about and that we should concentrate on our journey.

In the evening at 9.45pm on Thursday, we set off for Bangladesh. Our flight initially stopped at Delhi and then proceeded to its final destination, Dhaka where we stayed overnight because it was too late to travel any further. My wife's maternal uncle, Abdul Hamīd came to pick us up from Dhaka and on Saturday we travelled to our hometown Sylhet. My in-laws were dropped off on the way.

Due to my grandfather passing away, we immediately went to my maternal grandfather's village, Akil Pūr to visit what was now sadly, only his grave. My mother was utterly grief-stricken when she came to hear the heart-breaking news. Her primary objective for the trip was to visit her beloved father due to his severe illness, so she was bitterly devastated. I, alongside all of our relatives, sympathised and consoled her.

Reunion in Bangladesh

Coming to Bangladesh after such a long time brought back many memories of my childhood. It had been so long that I could not recognise my relatives and nor could they recognise me! In fact, on meeting my eldest uncle, I asked him about his whereabouts and well-being, not knowing that I was in fact speaking directly to him! Out of sheer happiness for my concern, he shed tears and exclaimed, "I am your eldest uncle!"

For the next few weeks, I was acquainted with all the relatives and neighbours of my village. It was a special experience being reunited with everybody after a long time.

Tested by Scholars

News spread like wildfire that a young man, aged only 21 years, who is a qualified Hāfiz, Qāri, Ālim and Mufti, had arrived in Bangladesh! Scholars approached me and in order to test my knowledge, they put forward many intricate Mas'alahs. I initially declined, explaining that I was only a student and anything they had heard about me regarding any qualifications and high status was not true. However, they would not have any of it!

One night, some scholars came and began asking me questions regarding the Tafsīr of the Holy Qur'ān. One particular question was: Why is 'Bismillāh' not mentioned before Sūrah Barā'ah? I gave them a few reasons mentioned in the books of Tafsīr which I had studied. They were surprised and impressed and they requested me to lead Jumu'ah (the Friday prayer) the following day.

I accepted the invitation and the next day, I was privileged to lead Jumu'ah in one of the local Masjids. As I was delivering the Khutbah (sermon), people stood up all of a sudden from the back to find out who I was. After the prayer, people flocked around me and hugged and embraced me. Thereafter, requests flooded in from all corners for me to visit different Masjids and Madrasahs.

Tarāwīh Salāh in Bangladesh

During my stay in Bangladesh, I visited many of the famous institutes there. One of these was Dārul-Qur'ān in Banyachong which was run by my father-in-law, Mufti Tālib Uddīn Ahmad Sāhib ﷺ. It was the month of Ramadhān and because I was Hāfiz-e-Qur'ān (memoriser of the Holy Qur'ān), everyone was eager to listen to my recitation.

I was requested to lead the Tarāwīh Salāh in the Masjid of Banyachong. I remember reciting the 15th Juz (part) and by the grace of Allāh ﷻ, I managed to complete it without any mistakes. In spite of this, there was unfortunately a Hāfiz who wanted to make the people think that I had made a mistake. Thus, he corrected my recitation by reciting an isolated verse.

This incident brought to light the fact that if I was to continue in this manner, there would be a degree of jealousy building up in the hearts of some of the people. Hence, it helped me to be more aware and conscious of this potential danger. After the Tarāwīh Salāh, people crowded around to shake hands with me and to request for Du'ās.

Salāh In Jamā'at – An Amazing Incident

In my final year at Dārul-Uloom Bury, all of the Bukhāri students performed I'tikāf. In my 40 days spiritual course, we would strive to perform our 5 daily Salāh with Takbīr– Ūlā (the opening Takbīr of the Imām). Alhamdulillāh, I had continued this noble practise after my graduation also.

During my visit to Bangladesh, I was once travelling to my uncle's village in a taxi with my grandmother, mother, maternal aunt and uncle. Whilst on the journey, the time for Asr Salāh approached. I requested the driver to stop nearby a Masjid so that I could perform my Salāh but to my surprise, he declined. As the time of Asr Salāh approached its end time, I feared that I would miss my Salāh so I insisted that he stop. However, this message just fell on deaf ears.

All of a sudden, the car abruptly stopped! The driver tried his best to re-start the car but to no avail. I could not believe that when I looked around, I noticed a Masjid nearby and the locals were performing their Asr Salāh! Hurriedly, I left the car and joined the congregation with the opening Takbīr. I was overjoyed and expressed my gratitude to Allāh ﷻ for allowing me to continue upon my practise of performing the Salāh with the Takbīr-Oola. After the Salāh, there was a Janāzah (funeral) and the people appointed me to perform the Janāzah Salāh.

When I completed the prayer, I came back to the car to find the driver still occupied in trying to repair the car. I got in and requested him to drive on. He tried the engine once more and to our utter amazement, the car re-started! I just smiled at him and praised Allāh ﷻ. When we arrived at my uncle's village, the news had already reached his ears that I had performed a Janāzah Salāh in a miraculous way! I seized the opportunity to explain to my uncle about the importance of Salāh.

Whilst in Bangladesh, I would deliver lectures in the Bangla language which was something new to me. I was encouraged and motivated by my relatives to speak and guide the people in matters of Dīn (religion). I realised sadly, that many of my own relatives did not even know the basics of Islām and I tried to explain to them the importance of seeking knowledge. I gathered all my cousins and encouraged them to study the Dīn and assured them that I would financially back them if they wanted to enrol into an Islamic institute.

Political Unrest

One day, during our travels, we got caught in a rally of two of the main political parties – BNP and Awwami League – who were stood face to face in a confrontation. Suddenly, to our horror, violence erupted and stones and bricks were being thrown all over the place! We swiftly had to take refuge in a nearby Hindu village for safety and remained there until the violence subdued. Alhamdulillāh, without any further delay, we returned back to our village safely. However, due to the political unrest in the country, there were frequent strikes and we could not fly back home at our fixed date. Our departure date was delayed by 10 days due to these political problems.

Second Journey to Bangladesh

In the year 2004, after severe flooding had taken place in Bangladesh, I had been contemplating on visiting the country myself to observe the condition of the flood affected areas and the people. However, it was the closing days of the academic year at JKN and Kitābs had to be finished. Hence, taking a break for the trip was difficult to accommodate. I had to make swift preparations.

Initially, I planned to travel on Monday the 13th of September for the two revision weeks prior to exams at JKN but due to the peak season, there were no seats available. Mufti Junaid, my brother-in-law, also decided to travel with me and he booked both of our tickets for Saturday the 4th of September 2004. As it was an earlier date, it meant that I had to dedicate my few remaining days in the UK to my teaching. Remarkably, I had to complete 3 and a half Juz of Jalālayn Tafsīr in just 2 days!

Amazing Completion of Jalālayn

On the 30th of August 2004, it was a Bank Holiday and I called all of the Mishkāt students to arrive at 12pm, so that we could derive maximum benefit from the time. Thus, the class arrived and by the grace of Allāh ﷻ, that day, after over 7 hours, three Juz were completed! The remaining half a Juz was completed the following day.

To celebrate this extraordinary accomplishment, one of my students, Dr Ibrāhīm Dadibhai, invited the class to a lavishing dinner in which samosas, kebabs, keema, chicken, meat, fish, vegetables, salad, drinks and lassi were served! This special dinner was held at my residential place, 118 Manningham Lane at 11pm and it was a wonderful and memorable occasion. Everybody was full of praises of Allāh ﷻ for granting the Tawfīq (ability) to have completed the entire Tafsīr of the Holy Qur'ān in grand style!

The Journey

As my departure day came closer, I became more and more busy, which had become a norm for me prior to taking journeys. On Friday the 3rd of September, I bid farewell to my mother, brothers, sisters, relatives, colleagues, friends and students and came home to prepare for the trip. However, every time I began packing there would be a phone call or a guest arriving to bid me farewell!

Eventually, I managed to complete my preparations and after bidding farewell to my wife, children and close students who had stayed awake all night with me, I set off at 4:30am with Maulāna Abū Tāhir Sāhib, the Imām of Shāh-Jalāl Masjid in Leeds and one of his Masjid Musallīs (worshippers), who were both travelling with me. Then my close colleague and travel companion, Hāfiz Azīzur-Rahmān Sāhib took the three of us to Oldham, where we halted to perform Fajr Salāh in Jamā'at and had a light snack and tea. From Oldham, we travelled to Manchester Airport, taking my brother-in-law, Mufti Junaid with us.

We boarded our flight from Manchester Airport to Heathrow Airport at 8:45am. After 35 minutes, we landed at Heathrow Airport where there was a waiting period of 4 hours before our next flight to Bangladesh, via Bimān Airlines, which was due for 2pm. In that duration of waiting, I decided to utilize the time by briefly writing about my travel experiences. We boarded onto the plane at 1:30pm and it commenced its journey at its appointed time. Before the departure, we performed our Zuhr Salāh in the prayer hall of Heathrow Airport. Asr, Maghrib and Ishā were performed in Jamā'at inside the plane, Alhamdulillāh. The flight lasted for 9 hours and at approximately 11:00pm and 5:00am local time, we landed at the Zia International Airport in Dhaka.

Due to the recent floods in the country, we thought that we may experience delays at the airport but Alhamdulillāh, there were no problems. At Zia International Airport, we performed our Fajr in the Airport prayer hall and a light breakfast and tea were served to all the passengers travelling by transit flight. We boarded on the plane for the domestic flight to Sylhet at 7:30am and after a short flight of 30 minutes, we landed at Osmani International Airport.

Arrival in Sylhet

Many people had come to the airport to welcome us including Maulāna Burhān Uddīn, the younger brother of Maulāna Āshiqur-Rahmān - a great Muhaddith, Maulāna Sharīf Uddīn, an old classmate of Mufti Junaid Sāhib and a talented and hardworking young scholar, Abdul Hamīd, my wife's maternal uncle, Monuhar Ali, my paternal uncle, Arab Ali, my maternal uncle and other scholars, students and well-wishers. Customs at the airport only took a few minutes; thus, we were swiftly out of the airport.

Before setting off for Biswanath, my home town, we briefly stopped at two places: Mufti Junaid's in-laws' residence for some tea and dinner and then, it was Maulāna Abū Tāhir Sāhib's stop, so we bid farewell to him. Maulāna Sharīf and others continued the journey with us to Duhal – the village in which I was born and had spent nearly seven years of my life.

Due to the severe floods, we travelled about 1 mile from the main roads to the village on boats, which was a new experience for me. My aunts, uncles, cousins and especially my paternal grandmother, who was nearly 100 years old, were waiting in anticipation to see me, so when I arrived it was a joyous occasion. After the warm reception, I managed to take some much needed rest. I spent the next day meeting my relatives and enquiring about their health and circumstances etc.

Visit to Two Great Institutes

On Monday 5th September, I visited the two famous Islamic Institutes in Biswanath. The first was Jāmiah Madania which was established over 40 years ago by the great scholar Shaykh Ashraf Ali Sāhib Biswanathi ﷺ, Former President of Jamiatul Ulamā Bangladesh. We were fortunate enough to meet the principal and also the staff of the Madrasah. The second Madrasah was Jāmiah Muhammadiyah which was established in 1990 by the great scholar Shaykh Sādiqur-Rahmān Sāhib ﷺ. Though Shaykh Sādiq ﷺ was not present at the time, we managed to meet and benefit from the

Shaykhul Hadīth of the Madrasah, Shaykh Abdul Malik Sāhib, and there was a very warm reception from all of the staff. I was taken around both the institutes and was very impressed by the standard of education as well as the buildings.

Invitation to All

My uncle Mohram Ali who lives in Coventry, UK was also in Bangladesh at the time. When he heard of my visit, he invited all the village people to a huge feast on the following Monday. Hundreds of people arrived at our village from morning till dusk. Mufti Junaid, Maulāna Sharīf and I ate with the local scholars.

Enquiries into Charity Work

One of my main objectives of my visit to Bangladesh was to observe the progress of Jāmia Zakariya Madrasah and Masjid Zakariya which I had decided to establish in my village. I met with the engineer and we discussed the work done so far and the work which was remaining. Alhamdulillāh, I was very pleased with the progress. I then visited the building site and met all of the workers and spoke to them regarding the importance of Salāh and ensuring the correction of their intentions when partaking in the construction of such a noble project.

After this, I had a meeting with my uncle Monuhar Ali regarding the progress and the finances. I was delighted to see the precise and minute detail regarding every penny spent so far for the construction work. In this meeting, I also discussed with my uncle regarding Al-Kawthar Welfare Foundation and about our intention to provide charity for the poor and needy. He generated a list of those people who were in need of help. Out of the 100 families he put forward, he selected a portion of them who were living in extreme poverty and I requested him to distribute relief aid to them. There were also a few families who needed emergency shelter and clean water, so I told my uncle to fulfill their needs with financial assistance.

Travelling to Various Villages—Akil Pūr

In Akil Pūr, I took the opportunity to visit the grave of my beloved maternal grandfather, Abdul Jabbār. Thereafter, we bid farewell to all of the relatives and set off for Banyachong.

Banyachong

Banyachong is a huge village which has transformed into a town with 15 unions. It is a beautiful and elegant place and it is the hometown of my wife's maternal uncles. In Banyachong, I visited Dārul-Qur'ān, the Madrasah of my late father-in-law, Mufti Tālib Uddīn Sāhib ﷺ. By this time, the Madrasah had progressed immensely with 550 students and 21 staff members.

Dārul-Qur'ān is one of the few Madrasahs in which the students are educated regarding the true spirit of Islām. I had the opportunity to meet the staff and listen to the recitation of the students. I was greatly impressed by the Qirāt, due to their correct Tajwīd and beautiful tone.

The staff were very co-operative, kind and hardworking and the students were busy preparing for their annual exams. I went to each class individually and spoke briefly to all the students regarding their studies, encouraging them to aim for the best. One thing which immensely impressed me was that the students were very dedicated to their books. I was amazed to see that throughout my tour around the institute, I did not observe a single student who was messing about or sitting idly.

Modhukhani

I went on to visit Modhukhani where I stayed two nights. Modhukhani was the home of the late maternal grandfather of my wife, Qāri Abdul Qādir, a famous renowned Qāri who achieved the gold medal in the whole of the Sylhet division for his recitation. He taught Qirāt to thousands of students over a period of 40 years. He passed away at the age of 95 on the 5th of June 2004. After Fajr on Wednesday 8th September, we visited his grave.

Satayhāl and Tājpūr

The next day, we set off early to Satayhāl, Nabigonj, a town within the district of Habigonj. Satayhal is the hometown of my father-in-law. Here, we visited the graveyard of my father-in-law's father, who was a prominent scholar of his time.

From there, our next destination was Tājpūr which was about 10km away. Maulāna Abū Tāhir Sāhib had established a Madrasah in Tājpūr. It was his earnest wish that I visit his Madrasah and perform the opening of the Masjid. There were many scholars, students and local residents waiting in anticipation for our arrival. I spent the night engaged in lengthy discussions with the scholars and we slept only a few hours.

The next day, I spoke before the Jumu'ah Salāh and then led the Jumu'ah Salāh and Khutbah. Maulāna Rūhul Amīn, a Muhaddith of Golmokafon Madrasah and an eminent and talented scholar, also addressed the gathering. Maulāna Rūhul Amīn is the son-in-law of Maulāna Abdul Alīm - my wife's maternal uncle. In this way he was my brother-in-law. I deeply admired his character, knowledge and piety.

Bolorampūr

After Jumu'ah and lunch we headed for Molvi Bazār accompanied by Maulāna Abū Tāhir. We reached Bolorampūr at about Maghrib time. It was my long yearning desire to visit this place and when I arrived, everyone came out in joy and happiness.

Shaykh Muhammad Ali - the great Khalīfah of Shaykh Husain Ahmad Madani ﷺ, was there waiting in anticipation for us. Shaykh was physically disabled and partially paralyzed and there were two students assisting him everywhere. He expressed great affection and love for me and he remarked, "My heart was yearning to see you." These words were so emotional that they brought tears to my eyes. Just to shake hands with the likes of pious saints like the Shaykh was a great honour for me. However, he spoke to me for a considerable amount of time, making me overjoyed to be in his honourable company. Food was served and was of many varieties, leaving me spellbound by the hospitality which I will never forget.

Too Many Invitations!

That evening, we were invited to Borūna, a village which became world famous due to the great saint, Shaykh Lutfur Rahmān, an eminent saint and pious sage. He was the great senior disciple of Shaykh Husain Ahmad Madani 🌺. Shaykh Lutfur Rahmān passed away on Tuesday 17th of May 1977 and from my childhood, I had the yearning to visit his village and grave.

At this point, it came to my knowledge that the relatives of my beloved teacher, Maulāna Abdul Jalīl Sāhib, had sacrificed a goat in which they planned to feed us for supper that evening. However, because we had already accepted the invitation at Borūna, we had no choice but to decline the invitation, although I felt extremely uneasy in refusing their kind gesture.

Borūna

After bidding farewell to the many scholars and residents, Maulāna Wali-ur-Rahmān, the brother-in-law of Maulāna Abdul Jalīl Sāhib, took us to Borūna. The first thing I did was visit the grave of Shaykh Lutfur Rahmān 🌺. I felt a great spirituality in my heart and Shaykh's youngest son, Maulāna Wali-ur-Rahmān went beyond the limits in hospitality and affection towards us. We also met the other sons of the Shaykh and spent some time with his eldest son, Maulāna Khalīl-ur-Rahmān, who is at present the principal and Shaykh in place of his father. Maulāna Khalīl-ur-Rahmān has many disciples in Britain and Bangladesh. One of the Shaykh's sons, Maulāna Saeed-ur-Rahmān, who invited us for breakfast, was a personality whom I had known for the last ten years due to his visit to the UK in 1996. Here in Bangladesh, during this visit, he was overjoyed to see me. We also met the Shaykh's prominent son, Mufti Fārūq Sāhib who established Jāmiah Madania, another Madrasah near Borūna.

After spending Friday night in Borūna we set off for Banyachong. On the way, Mufti Fārūq Sāhib invited us to his Madrasah. I was deeply impressed by the piety, character and hospitality of Mufti Fārūq Sāhib who honoured us so excessively. Maulāna Abū Tāhir Sāhib, Mufti Junaid and I addressed the students and teachers at his Madrasah and we were able to observe the teaching methods there. Everybody welcomed us with great zeal and jubilance and many honourable words were said to us. After performing Du'ā and writing a short reference for the Madrasah, we continued on our journey to Banyachong.

The next day, I had a much needed rest whilst Mufti Junaid went with Maulāna Sharīf and our driver Rubel to Sylhet to confirm our return tickets back to the UK for the 24th of September 2004.

Sunamgonj

The following day, we had a program exclusively for scholars in Sunamgonj which was very well organized by Maulānā Bahā Uddīn. The program was scheduled for 12pm but due to the damaged roads, we arrived late at 1:30pm.

Initially, we performed our Zuhr Salāh and then, Maulānā Abū Tāhir, Mufti Junaid and I addressed the enthusiastic gathering of approximately 200 scholars. I began by expressing my apology for the delay. I then praised and thanked Allāh ﷻ for allowing us to gather and for giving me the opportunity to meet so many scholars. I expressed my inability to speak in Bengali due to my education being imparted in the UK. My speech was concluded by a Du'ā and then food was served. After the gathering in Sunamgonj, we rushed back to Banyachong to stay the night there.

Mymensingh

Our next destination was Mymensingh, the home town of our colleague Maulānā Sharīf Uddīn. Maulānā Sharīf was a colleague and classmate of my brother-in-law, Mufti Junaid and he had taken a three week vacation to host our trip and take us around the various places. It was his yearning desire that we visit his poor district.

Alhamdulillāh, my cousin brother, Rubel was a very skilled driver and he managed all our travel needs from the day we landed at Sylhet airport. He was prepared to take us to Mymensingh though he was not certain regarding the route or how long the journey would be.

A Land of Natural Beauty ⸻ Mymensingh

We set off for our journey to Mymensingh at 9.30am and estimated that we would be travelling for approximately 6 hours. However, we travelled for hours and hours, yet still we had not reached to our destination. Eventually, we reached Netrokhuna, the small district of Mymensingh at 6pm. After performing Maghrib Salāh and having dinner, we travelled for a further hour or so. Then we halted and after parking our van in a safe place, we continued our journey by boat. By this time, it was very dark and it was a new experience for me to travel for so long. After two hours on the boat, we reached dry land. Here, two rickshaws were ready, waiting for us. We eventually reached our destination at 11pm after 13 long hours of travelling! Many brothers were there waiting for us and they had been anticipating our arrival since the morning. We met the brothers and briefly spoke to the attendees. After supper and Ishā Salāh, we retired to bed.

The following day, we walked around the flood affected area of Sirāmpur, which was the village of Maulāna Sharīf. The flood was so severe that it left many houses demolished, wrecked and damaged. We shared the grief and concern with the people and were deeply moved by their love and affection.

After Zuhr, we met the local scholars and briefly spoke to the gathering. The local scholar, Maulāna Luqmān introduced me with a very high profile, which I definitely did not deserve. Nevertheless, I emphasized to them the importance of establishing elementary schools to educate children from a young age. After the gathering, food was served by the host to all the attendees.

A Special Wedding

For some time, Mufti Junaid and I were encouraging our colleague Maulāna Sharīf to get married. He finally accepted and here in Mymensingh, he went to visit his future in-laws with Mufti Junaid and Maulāna Luqmān. Mufti Junaid and I took on the responsibility to assist him financially in his wedding. The Nikāh took place the next morning after Fajr with simplicity and basic food. It was a wonderful and simple wedding to remember!

Work of Al-Kawthar Welfare Foundation

By the grace of Allāh ﷻ, through Al-Kawthar Welfare Foundation, thousands of people have directly or indirectly benefitted, including scholars, students of Dīn, men, women and children.

Alhamdulillāh, Al-Kawthar has been able to establish two institutes of learning in Bangladesh. The first being Jāmiah Zakariyya, in my home village, Duhal, Biswanath, Sylhet and the second, Jāmiah Al-Kawthar, in the poor region of Netrokhuna. Alongside these, several Makātib (elementary schools) which are run in the morning, teaching basic Islamic education, have also been introduced in different parts of Bangladesh. Also, through Al-Kawthar's student sponsorship project, over 50 students have become Hāfiz-e-Qur'ān, by the Grace of Allāh ﷻ.

Hundreds of small homes have also been constructed for people who had no shelter at all. Furthermore, approximately 100 tube wells were planted around the whole of Bangladesh, providing clean water for those who previously had no access to clean water.

Once, when relief workers were distributing sheets of metal to people to use as shelter, there was a woman who fell to the ground sobbing as she received her sheets. Everyone was shocked to see her so upset. After all, this should have been a moment of happiness! When people enquired as to why she was crying, she replied, "I am crying out of joy! I never dreamt that I will ever live under a proper shelter! Thanks to Mufti Sāhib!" Subhān-Allāh!

In another place, during my visit to Bangladesh, an old woman invited me to her home for a meal. When I entered, she presented me with a single glass of water saying, "This is my invitation to you. It is the first time I am drinking fresh clean water, thanks to Al-Kawthar." How happy I was to be partaking in an invitation which was so basic yet contained so much Barakah! Alhamdulillāh! May Allāh ﷻ reward greatly all of our sponsors and donors and may He give us the ability to continue to do the work for the charity. Āmīn!

Third Journey to Bangladesh

My Re-Visit to Bangladesh and the Fatal Accident

For a few years we were involved in the work of Al-Kawthar Welfare Foundation in Bangladesh and at the end of March in 2009, I decided to visit the country to observe the charity work taking place there. I set off for this fateful journey from Birmingham Airport via Emirates Airlines, accompanied by my colleague, Maulāna Zubair Sūfi and my student, Mujībur-Rahmān. We were to meet my brother in-law, Mufti Junaid in Bangladesh as he was travelling on a different flight.

When we landed at Dhaka Airport, many colleagues and well-wishers had come to welcome us. We travelled to many places in Bangladesh, visiting and observing the many Islamic institutes over there. During these eventful days, I delivered many lectures, therefore, I hardly had any sleep or rest. Nevertheless, invitations were still flooding in from all corners of Bangladesh!

It was the fateful day on Saturday 4th April 2009, when after Fajr, I conducted a Dars (lesson) of Bukhāri Sharīf in Dārur-Rashād Madrasah (a famous institute which was founded by Shaykh Abul-Hasan Ali Nadwi ؒ). After the Dars, I was shown around the various departments of the institute. I was especially impressed with the language department in which students were able to deliver speeches fluently in Arabic, English, Urdu and Bangla.

After this, Shaykh Junaid Al-Habīb, a prominent lecturer in Bangladesh, invited me to visit his institute, Qāsimul-Ulūm. Due to the lack of time, this visit was reduced to a mere few minutes, after which, I consumed a quick breakfast, then swiftly set off for our next journey to visit Netrokhuna, which was a drive of over eight hours.

An Unusual Dream

We began our journey from Dhaka at approximately 10:00am and then halted at a service station to perform our Zuhr Salāh. The most peculiar thing happened at this service station. My student, Mujībur-Rahmān approached me to inform me that his mother had told him that she had seen a dream in which we had an accident. Mujībur-Rahmān suggested to me that we should not travel further, bearing in mind the dream. I pondered over the situation and came to the conclusion that we could not postpone our journey based on a mere dream. Therefore, I replied to him, "Pray to Allāh ﷻ for our safe journey." However, Allāh ﷻ, the Best of planners had another plan for us.

We continued with our journey towards our final destination, Netrokhuna. Due to extreme fatigue from my busy schedule of the previous days, I fell asleep on the way. I was fast asleep in the van when all of a sudden, to my utter astonishment and horror, I heard my colleagues and people outside shouting and shrieking! I could hear people with voices full of panic, screaming that we had an accident! I thought it was all just a nightmare as I was still drifting in between sleep and wakefulness. However, with a big jerk, I woke up and looked back to realise with utter shock that we were no longer on the road...

My eyes grew wide and my breath caught in my throat for I was being plummeted around in the van as it began tumbling into a ditch! Everybody was terrified and shocked and there was a strange silence as we were all rendered speechless. My student, Mujībur-Rahmān broke the silence with a fearful voice, "Ustād, we are going!" I turned my face towards him and saw blood gushing forth from his forehead. Seeing his distress, I took my hand and placed it on his forehead and said in an emotional voice, "Don't worry Mujībur-Rahmān, recite the Kalimah and all the rest of you brothers. If we are departing from this temporary abode, then let us go with Imān!" I then recited the Kalimah.

A Second Strange Incident

At this critical time, a second strange thing occurred. My mobile phone began to ring and as I pressed the button to answer the call, I heard the trembling voice of my beloved mother echoing, "My beloved son, have you had an accident? Are you ok?" I answered, "Yes mum, we have had an accident but we are ok. But how did you know?" She replied, "I woke up suddenly after seeing a dream in which I saw that you had an accident. So I insisted Rehāna (my youngest sister) to call you."

I was amazed at this because in England, it was only 9:00am in the morning of Saturday and this was a very unusual time for her to be phoning. After terminating the phone call, I became unconscious and subsequently, had no idea what was happening. Allāh ﷻ knows best what happened in that interim because sadly, people were seen crowded over us and our mobile phones were stolen from our injured bodies.

Regaining Consciousness

When I gained consciousness, I thought that I had left this world and gone to the next abode. I could not recognise anything. I thought about what I could present to my Allāh ﷻ that would gain for me my salvation. I pondered deeply but could think of nothing! I began to cry with regret but then, all of a sudden, I remembered something with which I could comfort myself, "O' Allāh ﷻ, I present the JKN institute as my means of salvation. Please accept it!"

After some time, I woke up hearing sounds of sobbing, screaming and shouting. I realised that I was in a hospital bed surrounded by nurses and doctors. My colleagues gazed towards me with tearful eyes. It was a painful encounter.

My Concern for Salāh

For the first time, I recognized that I could not move. My bones and ribs were moving from one side to another. I was motionless on my stretcher bed. Suddenly, I asked somebody to bring me a stone. He asked me the reason for such a strange request. I responded, "The sun is nearly setting, I need to perform my Asr Salāh with Tayammum." He looked at me with utter amazement and shock and exclaimed, "Mufti Sāhib, we are worried about your life and you are worried about your Salāh!?" I promptly replied, "Yes brother, I do not want to meet my Lord with a Salāh Qadhā (debt) on my head." So they brought me a stone and I wiped my face and hands with it. I then performed my two Rak'āt Qasr of Asr Salāh lying on the stretcher. Only then was I relieved and content.

A Special Visitor

Whilst I was in hospital, news of my accident gradually began to spread to every corner of Bangladesh and abroad. One old woman, in a state of panic and shock, entered into the hospital and enquired, "Where is Mufti Sāhib Hudhūr? Is he alive?! Is he ok?!" Frantically, she went from bed to bed, searching for me. When she was eventually directed towards my bed, she looked at me with tears in her eyes and taking a deep sigh, said, "Alhamdulillāh, everything is ok then."

By Allāh, I had no idea who this woman was or what had prompted her to come! I was told that she was one of our recipients of the Al-Kawthar Welfare Foundation. I was amazed and rendered emotional by her visit. It reminded me of the time at the Battle of Uhud, when a woman Sahābi was informed that her father, brother and son had all been martyred in the battle. Her reaction was to run out to enquire about the safety of the Holy Prophet ﷺ. Though she had lost so many family members, she was more concerned about the well-being of the Holy Prophet ﷺ! Subhān-Allāh! When she saw him, she exclaimed, "All calamities are easy after seeing the Holy Prophet ﷺ!"

Assessment of Injuries

Out of all the people who had been in the accident, I was the most severely injured. My student, Mujībur-Rahmān had a shoulder injury and he was lying on the bed next to mine. Within hours, the hospital became overcrowded with scholars, students and well-wishers. There were scholars who had arrived from Dhaka and they decided that I should be admitted into Ibn Sinā Hospital - one of the top hospitals in Dhaka.

The doctors took a scan to ascertain the extent of my injuries. The results were not positive. It was at this point that I realised the seriousness of my wounds. The pain in my body was deeply intolerable and I was actually screaming out of pain continuously. I was given injection after injection to relieve the pain but it just continued to increase. I was unable to move and my life, for a moment, seemed to be coming to an end.

At this critical juncture, my colleague and cousin Maulāna Juhair took care of me. He remained at my side through thick and thin, 24 hours round the clock. His hospitality, care and affection reminded me of the affection of my mother.

Transfer From Hospital

I was in the hospital ward for a few days but being hospitalised in Bangladesh was not cheap. The bill ran into Lacs. Hence, after consultation with the senior scholars of Dhaka, I was transferred to

Shaykh Junaid Al-Habīb's institute, Qāsimul-Ulūm. Though I had left the hospital, the doctors continued to visit me with the relevant medicine and advice.

News by then, had spread far and wide and the Madrasah became a central point for many people to visit me. All of my relatives and well-wishers poured into Dhaka. There were extraordinary scenes of mixed emotions, hope, kindness and regret. In addition, 24 hours around the clock, there would be great scholars from around Bangladesh flocking into the institute. The air was filled with emotion, sentiments and affection.

Restlessness and Confusion of the People

Whilst I was bedridden in Dhaka, some misleading information was being relayed to the people. Not knowing the extent of my injuries, some people spread the news that I had become completely paralysed! Some received the information that I was now wheelchair bound for the rest of my life! During all of this, I would continue to reassure people who rang or came to visit. I would inform them that I was fine, Alhamdulillāh, and that they should continue to pray for me.

One of my close friends and students, Maulāna Ātif Anwar once phoned and begged, "Please Mufti Sāhib, inform me of your actual state of injury. There is so much confusion regarding it in the UK." I comforted him saying, "I'm completely fine. Convey the message to everyone." Unfortunately, the message did not seem to be passed on successfully.

Far-Sightedness of My Beloved Wife

My wife phoned me unexpectedly. To my surprise, she began asking me a very intricate and contradictory question, regarding a Hadīth of Bukhāri which I had taught before my accident. I was shocked and bewildered that even my own wife did not seem to comprehend my condition! Though I answered the question to the best of my ability, the thought would continue to dominate my mind that how could my wife be so oblivious, though she is so intelligent!? It was only later on, when I came back to the UK that I discovered the far-sightedness of my wife...

One day, she approached me and announced, "O' Abū Naeem! That day, when I asked you regarding the Hadīth of Bukhāri, I know for sure that you must have been startled but let me disclose the reason for it. The only purpose was to give me peace of mind that Allāh ﷻ had kept your intellect intact! Due to the fact that many false and mixed rumours had been spreading everywhere, I wanted to reassure myself that you were fully conscious and sober in terms of your intellect and memory! Alhamdulillāh, I cried out in happiness that you were ok!" I stared at her in utter amazement and became lost in deep thought. May Allāh ﷻ bless her life and increase her knowledge and intellect. Āmīn!

Hospitality and Kindness of Shaykh Junaid Al-Habīb

Whilst staying at the institute of Shaykh Junaid Al-Habīb, the degree of his hospitality and kindness was immeasurable! Not only was he accommodating a seriously injured patient, but he was also playing host to the multitudes of visitors. On a daily basis, dozens of people would eat from the Dastarkhān (table-cloth) of Shaykh Junaid Al-Habīb. There would be a variety of dishes, fruits, vegetables and drinks available there at all times. I was being spoon-fed by his son-in-law, Maulāna Kamāl and my colleague, Maulāna Juhair and all of this continued for over a fortnight. May Allāh ﷻ grant the Shaykh the best of rewards in this life and the next. Āmīn!

Arrangements to Return to the UK

After some time, plans were made for me to return home to the UK so that I could receive better treatment and care there. In my current state, there was a concern that I would not be allowed to travel. Therefore, I booked business class tickets on an Emirates flight, costing me over a thousand pounds. I was very apprehensive about travelling in my condition and it felt like it would be an impossible mission for me. I was completely unable to move by myself but my colleague, Maulāna Zubair Sūfi reassured me that he would assist me all the way home.

On the planned day of the journey, an ambulance was booked to take me to the Airport. However, to everyone's shock, at this particular juncture, all of a sudden, my condition severely deteriorated. I was in acute pain, I could not tolerate it and I was fearful that travelling would be too difficult for me, so I refused to take the journey. I requested my brother-in-law to call my wife, Marzia to Bangladesh so that she can look after me.

There was chaos amongst my colleagues and well-wishers. Although they were saddened to part with me, they knew that it was for the best that I go home. They began to cry, pleading with me, "Please Mufti Sāhib! Try your best! You need to go to the UK for your treatment!" I was in severe pain and I was completely confused. I did not know what to do. Therefore, I did the only thing that I could, which was to place my trust completely upon Allāh ﷻ having hope that He would help me. I indicated to the people to proceed towards the airport.

At the airport, the people bid farewell to me by embracing and kissing my forehead, all the while sobbing and weeping. I was so moved by their sentiments and the demonstration of pure brotherhood, that I could not hold back my own tears and I sobbed out of love and emotion.

An Unexpected Phone Call

On our way to the airport, there was a sister who phoned my colleague and pleaded to him to pass the phone on to me, so that she could speak to me. He explained to her that it was not an ideal time for me to talk. However, she persisted so my colleague held the phone at my ear and I asked who the sister was. The only reply I could hear was the sound of sobbing from the other end. After some time, she withheld her sobs and answered, "I am that unfortunate woman who could not fulfil the hospitality of a scholar of your calibre." Tears began to roll down my cheeks and I consoled her, explaining that she had done more than I ever expected or dreamt of.

Suddenly, another sister took the phone and a similar conversation was exchanged. I asked them both repeatedly who they were and eventually, they replied, "We are the two wives of Shaykh Junaid Al-Habīb." Subhān-Allāh! How much they did for me and how humble they were regarding their tireless support! They ended the call requesting repeatedly for Du'ās. May Allāh ﷻ bless their lives and always keep them both happy and may Allāh ﷻ give them a befitting reward for their hospitality. Āmīn!

My Journey Back to the UK

When the airport officials saw me in a wheelchair with a neck collar and braces on my body, they took pity upon my condition. They immediately put me on the plane and throughout the journey, I was lying on a sofa, in the business class section, with very caring staff who took good care of me, Alhamdulillāh.

When I landed at Birmingham Airport, many colleagues came to receive me and a special car was hired by my two students – Maulāna Rizwān and Maulāna Irfān to take me back to Bradford as comfortably as possible. On reaching Bradford, it was past midnight but many people were still awake, waiting anxiously to see my condition.

My beloved mother caught one glimpse of me in the wheelchair and she immediately fainted. When she regained her senses, she sobbed uncontrollably, whilst grasping me in a hug.

Everybody was incredibly grieved to see me in my condition. I was taken to my bedroom on top of the shop and when news spread of my return, people began to flock. Due to the crowd of visitors, an announcement was made in the Masjid the next day, regarding visiting times. There was one time for the general public and one for scholars and students. Emotional and sentimental scenes were witnessed throughout the day.

My father-in-law was also critically ill at the time but despite this, he arrived in the morning to visit me. Seeing my pitiful condition, he cried like a child. Scholars, students, friends, colleagues and the general public could not hold back their tears during their visits. The whole time, I would comfort everyone, hiding my own tears, though deep down, my heart was also tearing.

Admission into Hospital

After consulting with my GP and colleague Maulānā Dr Rafāqat Rashīd, an ambulance was called on Thursday morning and I was admitted into the Bradford Royal Infirmary. All the necessary scans and medical checks were carried out, revealing the extent of my injuries. The reports showed that bones in my neck, ribs and back were broken and damaged. Furthermore, there were also major problems with my internal body. I was strictly instructed not to make any movements until the surgery took place.

That night, the doctors and surgeons were discussing the seriousness of my condition with the specialists at St. James Hospital in Leeds. They were trying to arrange a slot where they could carry out an emergency operation on my bones to re-structure them. Throughout the night I could hear them on the phone but nothing was finalised.

The following day, the consultant came and assessed my reports. He was not happy with what he saw, "This is a serious injury. We cannot say whether you will survive or not. It is possible that you will have a blood clot or develop Pneumonia. Your condition is very serious. Do you want us to call a Muslim Chaplain to sympathise with you?"

I took a deep sigh as it seemed that my life would be coming to an end. I pondered over my situation and remarked, "It's ok, I will sympathise with myself. All my life I have sympathised with people. It is time that for once, I sympathise with myself. I have my God, Allāh ﷻ Who will look after me. But one thing I would like to mention is, this accident took place nearly 3 weeks ago. If anything drastic or critical had to happen, it would have happened then. But I have high hopes in my Allāh ﷻ, that I will be ok."

The consultant stared at me in amazement and paused. He then exclaimed, "Yes, this is a brilliant point! You seem very intelligent." Then he scribbled down a lot of information on his file and told me to rest for the remainder of the day.

After Jumu'ah Salāh that day, special Du'ās were made for me in Tawakkulia Masjid and other Masājid across the UK. After the Jumu'ah Salāh, immediately people began rushing towards the hospital. There was a wave of people who had come from all across the UK including many relatives from London, Coventry, Oldham and Leeds. The hospital staff became uneasy and frustrated with the masses of people so they had to restrict the number of visitors. Many people who had travelled a long way to see me, were only afforded a quick glance and a wave of their hands, before having to leave due to the restrictions. I was still in bitter pain, so I would just look at everybody whilst replying to their Salāms. My wife and other relatives would take turns to remain by my side until night time.

Back Home

The next day, a nurse came and unexpectedly informed me that I would be sent home that day, after having my neck collar and braces put on. I was utterly amazed that I would be allowed home so soon, without needing surgery! I praised Allāh ﷻ and after the necessary care, I was driven home by an ambulance. My family, relatives, friends and local residents were astonished and they asked why I was sent home so quickly. I replied, "I do not know. Only Allāh ﷻ knows!"

During my stay in the hospital, it was a unique experience to be staying with people who suffered from Dementia as I was unable to sleep throughout the night. Now I had the opportunity to rest properly. My close friend and colleague Waseem Rāja from Dewsbury (may Allāh ﷻ reward him greatly), kindly gifted me an electronic bed to assist me in my recovery, which I found very convenient, Alhamdulillāh. I would lie down on my bed without a pillow with the neck collar and braces fastened at all times.

When the people received the news of my return home, it was as though it had become the day of Eid for them! Throughout the day and night there would be continuous visitors coming and sympathising with me.

Fourth Journey to Bangladesh Via Saudi Arabia

Journey of a Lifetime

Visiting Makkah Mukarramah and Madīnah Munawwarah, no matter how many times we visit, is always a privilege, honour and a great fortune. After Hajj of 2016, I already planned to travel for 'Umrah in December 2016. Due to the increase in visa fees for frequent travellers, my colleagues advised me to drop 'Umrah from the full package and only proceed for the journey to Bangladesh. I was reluctant and explained that it does not matter how much fees has increased as I needed to perform my 'Umrah, because I had already consolidated my intention for 'Umrah with Bangladesh. They all agreed and my colleagues also agreed to pay the extra fees for 'Umrah.

Passport Issue

It so happened that when my passport was given to the Saudi Embassy for the 'Umrah visa, it was returned back because of the lack of pages in my passport. I was informed that passports required two empty pages consecutively to enable them to be stamped for Umrah visa. My passport was returned to me and I had to make an urgent appointment to renew it. The earliest appointment I was given was on Tuesday 6th December 2016 at 9:30am at the Liverpool passport office. I managed to get the passport on the same day and post it via special delivery to London. It was submitted on Thursday to the Saudi embassy and Alhamdulillāh, by the grace of Allāh ﷻ, I was informed that I received my visa after Jumu'ah.

My passport was picked up by my colleague Maulāna Ahmad Madani Sāhib and delivered to the house of Hāfiz Kawthar Sāhib who was coming to Bradford in the evening. Hāfiz Kawthar lived in St. Albans and was my friend from my Dārul-Ulūm Bury days. He had previously travelled with me to Hajj few months ago and was also accompanying me for 'Umrah alongside my other two colleagues, Maulāna Abdus-Salām Sāhib and Al-Hājj Dobir Miah Sāhib.

Up until 3pm Friday, I was unsure if I would be able to travel the next day. However, when my colleague Maulāna Abdus-Salām Sāhib rang me with the good news that I had received my visa, I had to make swift preparations. I contacted my brothers and sisters and bid them farewell. In the evening, I had classes till

10:30pm and managed to meet some of the staff and students.

After reaching home, I attended to all my financial matters including getting up to date with all the wages of the schools, JKN Institute and other employees. I only managed to sleep a couple of hours that night. In the morning, I woke up at 5:30am and after a quick light breakfast, lead the Fajr Salāh with my colleagues and well-wishers.

My close student and colleague, brother Dilwār volunteered to drive us to Manchester Aiport alongside Maulāna Habībur-Rahmān Sāhib, a JKN teacher. After bidding the family farewell, we set off at 7:00am from Bradford and reached Manchester Airport at 8:00am. My brother-in-law, Maulāna Tufayl was waiting in the airport to meet me with Maulāna Yahyā's son, Maulāna Tanwīr and his wife who were also travelling on the same flight. Also, Hāfiz Patel Sāhib's son, Maulāna Yūsuf Darwān and his entire family were travelling for 'Umrah and I was honoured to be in his company throughout the journey. Alhamdulillāh, we discussed different Fiqhi issues throughout the journey.

At this time, Manchester Airport was very busy which was most likely due to the Christmas period and people were leaving the country for a vacation. Our flight scheduled at 10:15am was delayed by an hour, but we had food and an enjoyable flight via Saudi airlines. Alhamdulillāh, we managed to perform our Zuhr, Asr and Maghrib Salāh in the plane in congregation with up to 10 people. This prayer facility is unique to the Saudi airlines which I had not previously seen with any other airlines. There was an exclusive prayer area for the air-flight passengers. May Allāh ﷻ reward the authorities for providing this facility for the Muslim travellers. Āmīn.

Madīnah Munawwarah

After the 6 hour flight, we landed at King Abdul-Azīz International Airport and surprisingly, our customs were very swift and organised. Within an hour, we were out from immigration and baggage collection. Our taxi was already pre-booked by our close colleague, Maulāna Abdur-Rahmān Sāhib who resides in Makkah Mukarramah.

For this 'Umrah, we decided to travel first to Madīnah Munawwarah and thereafter, wear the Ihrām from Dhul-Hulaifah, thus, we performed the 'Umrah, following in the footsteps of our beloved Prophet Muhammad ﷺ. Our taxi driver was a young, helpful and energetic individual who got us to our hotel, Jawharatul-Āsimah in Madīnah Munawwarah within 5 hours. After reaching our destination, we retired to bed after Fajr Salāh.

The blessed city of our beloved Prophet ﷺ always fascinates me with its serene, tranquil and peaceful environment. Within a few minutes, all my stress and fatigue disappeared. I felt at ease and commenced my recitation of the Holy Qur'ān and the compilation of my latest books, 'Protection from Black Magic' and 'Precious Pearls of the Holy Qur'ān'.

Another friend of mine, brother Rahīmullāh alongside his wife, his son Zakariyā, his mother in-law and his brother-in-law were staying in the same hotel as us. They were delighted to see me and my colleagues.

On Sunday, after Asr Salāh, we visited Baqī ul-Garqad – the graveyard of Madīnah Munawwarah which accommodates the blessed bodies of over 10,000 Companions of the Holy Prophet ﷺ, including the third Caliph, Sayyidunā 'Uthmān ؓ and the honourable wives of our beloved Prophet Muhammad ﷺ. In front of the grave of Sayyidunā 'Uthmān ؓ, I contemplated on his rich legacy and the sacrifice he went through for the elevation of Islām, to the extent that he even sacrificed his own life. His merciless murder flashed through my mind and heart and I could not hold back my tears. May Allāh ﷻ reward him and all the Companions of the Holy Prophet ﷺ the best of rewards. Āmīn.

A Land of Natural Beauty	Madīnah Munawwarah

Baqī-ul-Gharqad

After Ishā Salāh, we had supper and took some rest. At 2:00 am we visited the sacred grave of the Holy Prophet ﷺ, individually prayed 2 Rak'āt in Riyādul Jannah and recited the Holy Qur'ān.

Riyādh ul Jannah

As always, this was one of the highest privileges and honours that we were blessed to do the Ziyārah of the Holy Prophet ﷺ. May Allāh ﷻ accept our efforts and bring us to Madīnah Munawwarah again and again. Āmīn.

On Monday morning at 11am, we visited Masjid Qūba to fulfil the Sunnah of our beloved Prophet ﷺ of praying 2 Rakāt Salāh therein to achieve the reward of 'Umrah.

We also visited the area of the Battle of Uhud and sent our Salām upon the martyrs of Uhud, especially Sayyidush-Shuhadā, Sayyidunā Hamza ؓ and Sayyidunā Mus'ab Ibn-'Umayr ؓ.

A Land of Natural Beauty Makkah Mukarramah

Masid Qūba — Madīnah

Uhud

Alhamdulillāh, my two days in Madīnah Munawwarah were so peaceful that I spent most of my time engaged in the recitation of the Holy Qur'ān and proof reading my future compilations. It was precisely for this reason that I always looked forward to visiting Madīnah Munawwarah to achieve this peaceful and tranquil environment.

At night, we spent a considerable amount of time sending salutations on behalf of all our well-wishers, friends and relatives. Words cannot do justice to describe the scenario and the feeling which transpired through my mind and heart. May Allāh ﷻ bless us with His Noble Prophet's ﷺ Ziyārah again and again. Āmīn!

Makkah Mukarramah

On Tuesday 13th December 2016, after Zuhr Salāh, we set off for our 'Umrah towards Makkah Mukarramah. My close friend, brother Rahīmullāh, his wife and youngest child Zakariya, travelled with us in our van alongside his mother-in-law and brother-in-law. We halted at Dhul-Hulaifah to wear our Ihrāms and perform our Asr Salāh. At the next service station, we performed our Maghrib Salāh and within five hours, we reached Makkah Mukarramah. After a quick snack, we proceeded to complete our 'Umrah. Alhamdulillāh, we managed to perform our 'Umrah with ease and comfort within one and a half hours - all praise be to Allāh ﷻ.

At this point, my friend from my student days, Hāfiz Kawthar managed to sort out live streaming from our hotel Lu'Lu'-al-Sharq in the Haram. Hence I thought it would be worthwhile to teach our students of JKN. On Wednesday at 6:30pm UK time and 9:30pm Saudi Arabia time, I taught the translation of the Qur'ān via live streaming. It was a success by the grace of Allāh ﷻ. Later on, I also taught Mishkāt Sharīf for the English side and Urdu side students at 9:30pm UK Time and 12:30pm Saudi Arabia time.

In Makkah Mukarramah, I occupied myself with the recitation of the Holy Qur'ān and proof-reading my latest books. It was so peaceful and serene, similar to Madīnah Munawwarah. I utilised the night in Salāh and Tawāf with my colleagues. My timetable was as follows:

- Between Fajr and Zuhr – Sleeping time
- Between Zuhr and Asr – Compiling books
- After Asr Salāh - Recitation of the Holy Qur'ān
- After Maghrib Salāh - Study time and rest
- Between Ishā till Fajr - Tawāf and completing my Qur'ān recitation.

On Friday, we performed our Jumu'ah Salāh behind Shaykh Sudais, who spoke about the importance of Sabr (patience) and Du'ā for our oppressed brothers and sisters in Syria and other parts of the Muslim world. He explained that there is always wisdom in the actions of Allāh ﷻ and that Allāh ﷻ will ultimately bring success and happiness for the Muslims.

Shaykh Sudais drew a parable from the incident of the treaty of

Hudaybiah - that initially, the treaty seemed very destructive and problematic for the Muslims but ultimately it became a blessing in disguise. Upon the treaty, Allāh ﷻ revealed the verses of Sūrah Fath (Chapter of Victory).

Sayyidunā Umar ؓ questioned in surprise, "Is this (peace treaty) a victory?" The Prophet ﷺ replied, "Definitely it is!" History testifies how it materialised as the biggest success and victory for the Muslims. Subhān-Allāh!

In the evening, we decided to complete our Khatm-Qur'ān and I instructed the male and female teachers of JKN to complete Khatms of the Holy Qur'ān with all the students. We decided to broadcast a live Du'ā in JKN for the suffering Muslims of Syria at 8:00pm UK time. This message was broadcasted to all our contacts and Alhamdulillāh, it proved very beneficial. At 8:00pm UK time and 11:00pm Saudi time, all our colleagues gathered together in the Haram and we did the live streaming for all the listeners. In the beginning of my brief talk, I mentioned the importance of steadfastness and patience and mentioned that as Muslims, we should never become despondent from the Mercy of Allāh ﷻ. We should contribute our efforts in whatever capacity we can.

I also requested everyone to pray for our close and honourable Imām of Shāh Jalāl Masjid (Bradford), Maulāna Abdul-Haq Sāhib who passed away on Friday after Jumu'ah Salāh in Apollo Hospital, Dhaka. Maulāna was a very close friend of mine and was amongst the senior Imāms of Bradford – being the Imām of Shāh Jalāl Masjid for nearly thirty years.

Just before he was leaving for Bangladesh, he phoned me whilst I was in the UK and informed me regarding his departure to Bangladesh. He insisted that he meets me in person to bid me farewell. I told him not to inconvenience himself and that bidding farewell on the phone was sufficient, but he was persistent on meeting me face to face. Hence, just before leaving, he came to the Al-Mu'min Bookshop for his formal farewell. It was an emotional departure and he pleaded forgiveness for any short-comings on his behalf.

This was a great quality of Maulāna that he regarded everyone as his senior, even though I was his son's age. Maulāna had so much compassion towards me that whenever he wanted any advice, he would personally present himself in my office and invite me to his house for a meal and then ask for that particular advice. I could remember him practicing on this hospitality on many occasions. Whenever Maulāna wanted to invite me to his Masjid for a lecture, he would personally make an appointment according to my convenience and then present himself with his Masjid committee. Allāhu Akbar! What level of respect he had for people. This type of hospitality was not restricted to myself, rather I was informed this was his general approach with people of all walks of life.

Maulāna had 3 sons studying in JKN Madrasah. Māshā-Allāh, all his 3 sons, Sa'eed, Na'eem and Sāim are Hāfiz-e-Qur'ān, very obedient and possess similar qualities as their father. One of his two daughters is a member of staff at JKN, and the other is currently studying the Ālim class despite being a busy mother. May Allāh ﷻ make his children a Sadaqah-e-Jāriyah on his behalf and may He forgive the sins of Maulānā and elevate his ranks to the highest abode in Jannatul-Firdaus. Āmīn.

Prior to the Du'ā, I was suffering from influenza and a feverish cold, hence I was reluctant to conduct the live streaming. My illness was apparent in my talk and Du'ā and was noticed by many close students including my dear wife, Āpa Marzia in the UK. Nevertheless, the talk and Du'ā was broadcasted successfully without any electronic failure.

Alhamdulillāh, our JKN students and staff managed to complete over 15 Khatms of the Qur'ān and my colleagues and myself managed to complete a few Khatms in the Haram. By the grace of Allāh ﷻ, many brothers and sisters around the globe were able to listen and participate in the Du'ā with appreciation and many sent me positive feedback. May Allāh ﷻ accept our Du'ās on behalf of all the Muslims around the globe who are facing so much trials and tribulations at the hands of the oppressors and tyrants. May He make it sincerely for His pleasure and make it a means of salvation for every one of us. Āmīn.

At this point, I want to share an article which a senior student of JKN, Sister Sahla wrote whilst on my journey.

Prayer for Aleppo

In December 2016, the Muslim world was shaken by the horrific scenes of war in the town of Aleppo in Syria. Many women, children and elderly people were the victims of an onslaught of bombs by the corrupt leaders of the country and their allies. Muslims around the world were left feeling helpless as to what to do to help, despite being extremely grieved at the plight of their innocent brothers and sisters. Many such people were those in Bradford and staff and students of JKN.

At the time, it was the final week of studies before a two week break for holidays at the Madrasah and Mufti Sāhib had gone for 'Umrah for a week before heading for Bangladesh to do Da'wah work there during the Madrasah holidays.

Making the most of the modern technology available, Mufti Sāhib arranged for a special Du'ā to be made for the suffering Muslims in Syria, which he would perform live from the Haram Sharīf in Makkah Mukarramah, to be broadcasted at the Madrasah where all the staff and students had gathered. Furthermore, many people around the world, through social media were also able to listen and participate live.

Prior to the live Du'ā, the staff and students were given time out from lessons in order to recite the Holy Qur'ān and do Dhikr on behalf of the Syrian people. Thereafter, the live feed was broadcasted.

At the time, Mufti Sāhib was suffering from a flu and it could be heard in his voice but nevertheless, he continued on with the noble cause. He began by encouraging us not to despair of the situation and become despondent and inactive. He explained that we are nearing the end times in which such hardships would become prevalent but that we should always remember that this life is temporary and its problems are temporary. Thereafter, he performed a powerful, emotional and lengthy Du'ā on behalf of the suffering Muslims which did not leave a dry eye in the entire Madrasah.

Later, it was announced that altogether, 14 Khatms of the Holy Qur'ān were recited and over 3000 people across the globe participated in the Du'ā, by the grace of Allāh ﷻ. The staff and students felt some small sense of solace that something, even though very little, was done on behalf of the suffering Syrians.

It was hoped through the mercy of Allāh ﷻ due to the sanctity of the Haram Sharīf, Mufti Sāhib's blessed 'Umrah trip, the blessed gathering of teachers and students of Dīn in which Allāh's ﷻ words were being recited and many participants from around the world, that all this would contribute to drawing the Mercy of Allāh ﷻ, the Most Merciful of those who show mercy and help towards the alleviation of the suffering of the Muslims around the world. May Allāh ﷻ accept our efforts, no matter how small they are and may He accept our Du'ās for all the suffering Muslim brothers and sisters around the world. Āmīn!

Last Day of Term at JKN Madrasah

Friday 17th December 2016 was the final day of Madrasah before breaking up for the two weeks of winter holidays. Hence, I emphasised to our students to value each day and make it 'Holy-days!' Later on at 12:30am in Saudi Arabia, I taught the Mishkāt Sharīf from the chapter of knowledge. In one particular Hadīth, the Holy Prophet ﷺ mentions about a prophecy, where people will travel to all corners of the globe to seek knowledge and they will not find any scholar more knowledgeable than the scholar of Madīnah Munawwarah.

Sufyān Ibn-Uwaynah ﷺ, the great Muhaddith, is of the opinion that it refers to the great scholar Imām Mālik ﷺ. Under the commentary of the Hadīth, I mentioned the love Imām Mālik ﷺ had for Madīnah Munawwarah and the respect he had for Hadīth. These are our pious predecessors who we should emulate to attain the success of both worlds. May Allāh ﷻ give us the Tawfīq (ability).

After the live streaming, I went to perform Tawāf and complete the remainder of my of Sunnah and Witr Salāhs. On the following day, we packed up and got ready for the next chapter of our journey, Bangladesh.

A Land of Natural Beauty — Bangladesh

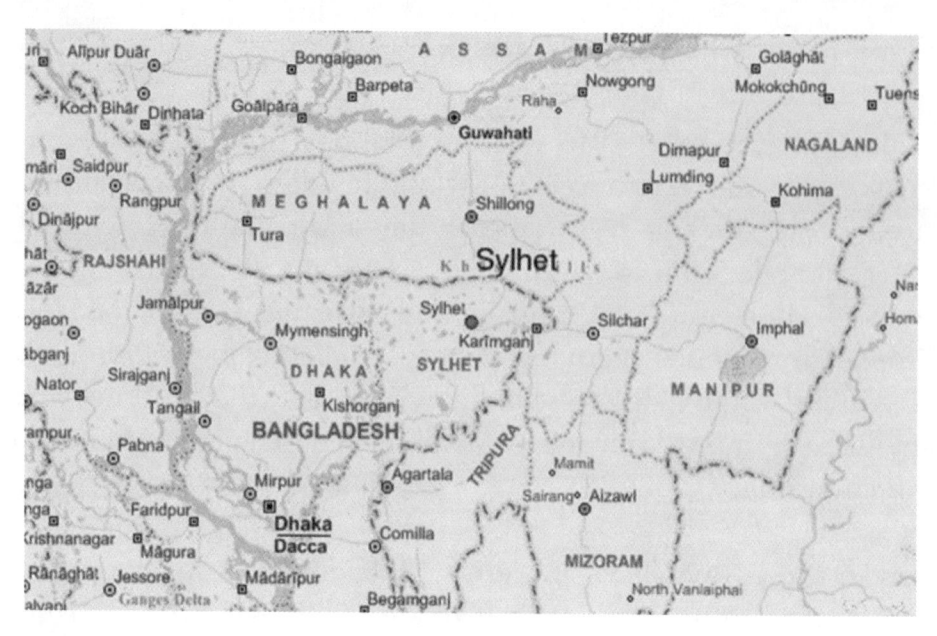

Bangladesh Map

Bangladesh

After performing our Asr Salāh, we proceeded towards King Abdul-Azīz Airport. After immigration procedures, our plane set off and five hours, thirty minutes later, it landed at Hazrat Shāh Jalāl International Airport at 7:45am. Due to the fact that I had no visa for Bangladesh, I had to obtain a month's visa on arrival which cost me just over 4000 Takas (£40). Alhamdulillāh, two army officers were there to assist us throughout which hastened the immigration procedure.

At the airport, our friends and colleagues were waiting anxiously to meet us. My cousin brother, Maulāna Abdul-Quddūs arrived the night before to Dhaka, while our other colleagues including Maulāna Juhair, Maulāna Sharīf-ud-Dīn and Maulāna Kamāl-ud-Dīn Sālih (the son in law of the famous scholar, Maulāna Junaid Al-Habīb) all arrived early in the morning.

Our first stop was the Madrasah of Maulāna Junaid Al-Habīb and after a heavy breakfast, we performed our Zuhr Salāh. Maulāna Junaid Al-Habīb gathered all the professional and English educated brothers and the students of the institute to whom I addressed in the English language. In my address, I explained the importance of implementing Dīn in every aspect of life, whether a person is a student of Madrasah or a student of a college or university. Islām is an all-embracing religion, fit for all types of people, at all times in every region of the world. I further explained to them the reward of practising upon the Dīn in the current volatile climate. Quoting the Hadīth:

يَأْتِيْ عَلَى النَّاسِ زَمَانٌ اَلصَّابِرُ فِيْهِمْ عَلَى دِيْنِهِ كَالْقَابِضِ عَلَى الْجَمْرِ

"A time will dawn upon the people when a person persevering on his Dīn will be like a person holding on a hot cinder." (Tirmizī)

The programme concluded with a Du'ā. Our supper and stay over was arranged in the residence of Maulāna Junaid Al-Habīb.

The following day, after breakfast we set off for my village in Biswanath, where we arranged an Islāhi (spiritual) programme. On the way, we halted in the town of Habigonj for dinner at Al-Hājj

Dobir Miah's house, which he had arranged well in advance from the UK. After reaching our village, I briefly met my relatives including my two paternal aunt's who were waiting in anticipation for my arrival. I lead Ishā Salāh, as a Muqīm (resident) in my village where I was born and lived for nearly 7 years of my life.

In my address to the congregation, who eagerly waited for my arrival, I briefly touched upon the purpose of the Islāhi programme. I elaborated on the Qur'anic verse,

$$\text{يَا أَيُّهَا الَّذِينَ آمَنُوا اتَّقُوا اللَّهَ وَكُونُوا مَعَ الصَّادِقِينَ}$$

"O you who believe! Fear Allāh and stay with the truthful" (9:119)

This verse teaches us how to achieve the friendship of Allāh ﷻ in a nutshell. In one of my previous lectures, which has now been published in a book called, 'How to Become a Friend of Allāh ﷻ' I elaborated on this verse in detail (please refer to the book for more information).

After the programme, I met local and eminent scholars including Maulāna Najmud-Dīn Qāsimi and Maulāna Mashāhid – two great scholars of the Sylhet district. Our food and stay over was scheduled in the village of Maulāna Lutfur-Rahmān Sāhib, who in my absence, runs our village institute, Jāmiah Zakariya. Alhamdulillāh, may Allāh ﷻ bless him, he diligently works towards the success of the institute as well as his own institute Jāmiah Lutfiya, Biswanath. The following day, after breakfast, we set off for Sorsondi, the village of Maulāna Abdus-Salām Sāhib. I was scheduled for a talk to the females in the area before Zuhr Salāh. Prior to my talk, Maulāna Hārith-ud-Dīn Sāhib addressed the sisters and then the principal of Jāmiah Muhammadiyah, Maulāna Habībur Rahmān Sāhib also addressed the gathering. After them, I spoke on the importance of rectification in our lives before it is too late and to adopt the habit of performing Salāh on time with punctuality.

After Asr Salāh, we headed for a Madrasah in the Biswanath town called Qurma, where they conduct a monthly Islāhi Majlis. For the audience, I touched on the mission of the Holy Prophet ﷺ which Allāh ﷻ highlights under the verse,

$$\text{لَقَدْ مَنَّ اللَّهُ عَلَى الْمُؤْمِنِينَ إِذْ بَعَثَ فِيهِمْ رَسُولًا مِنْ أَنْفُسِهِمْ يَتْلُو عَلَيْهِمْ آيَاتِهِ وَيُزَكِّيهِمْ وَيُعَلِّمُهُمُ الْكِتَابَ وَالْحِكْمَةَ}$$

"Indeed, Allāh ﷻ has showered His blessings upon the believers when He sent amongst them a Messenger who recites upon them the book, purifies them and teaches them the book and wisdom." (3:164)

I explained the mission of the Prophet ﷺ and how we should implement these qualities within ourselves. From Qurma, we came back to Jāmiah Abdullāh Ibn Umar ؓ for the annual Jalsa with my close colleague, Maulāna Abdus-Salām Sāhib within the time frame. Due to my visit last year for the same annual gathering, people already knew me, hence there were many familiar faces which I recognised. I spoke in details about true success in the eyes of Allāh ﷻ and how to achieve it. The Holy Prophet ﷺ states,

$$ اَلْكَيِّسُ مَنْ دَانَ نَفْسَهُ وَعَمِلَ لِمَا بَعْدَ الْمَوْتِ وَالْعَاجِزُ مَنْ أَتْبَعَ نَفْسَهُ هَوَاهَا وَ تَمَنّٰى عَلَى اللّٰهِ $$

"The intelligent person is the one who subdues his desires and works for the life after death and the foolish person is the one who follows his desires and has vain hopes in Allāh ﷻ." (Tirmizī)

I explained that this world is an illusion and merely a test for the real life of the Hereafter. The programme concluded with a Du'ā and then we retired to our sleeping quarters after a day of continuous programmes and travels. May Allāh ﷻ accept our endeavours and efforts and make it sincerely for His pleasure. Āmīn!

Wednesday 21st December 2016

In the morning, after breakfast, we set off for our scheduled programme in Patagoin Madrasah which I was a patron of. However, in between another Madrasah programme was included, at Amtoil Madrasah in Biswanath, where I addressed the students and staff. After Zuhr Salāh, I spoke to the students and staff of Patagoin Madrasah about the importance of forsaking evil traits in student days in order to be successful in later life after graduation. After the speech, all the staff of the institute, took the oath of allegiance with me for the progression of their spiritual life.

After Asr Salāh, we proceeded towards Misbāhul-Ulūm, Jointa, the

Madrasah of Maulānā Hārith-ud-Dīn Sāhib who had organised an Islāhi (spiritual) programme. After our arrival, I was ushered to their huge tent which was arranged for the large number of attendees. I highlighted upon the verse,

$$\text{يَٰٓأَيُّهَا ٱلَّذِينَ ءَامَنُوا۟ ٱتَّقُوا۟ ٱللَّهَ وَكُونُوا۟ مَعَ ٱلصَّٰدِقِينَ}$$

"O you who believe! Fear Allāh ﷻ and stay with the truthful." (9:119)

I explained briefly the connection between the three points, Imān, Taqwa and pious people and how important it is to search for pious companionship. After the gathering, a great number of scholars, local elders and youngsters took the oath of allegiance with me.

Shāmpūr, Joynta was the village where my father-in-law Mufti Tālib-ud-Dīn Sāhib ؒ married his second wife, and his second father-in-law was Maulānā Hārith-ud-Dīn Sāhib, who would continuously insist that I visit his Madrasah, especially after the demise of my father-in-law. I was overwhelmed with happiness and joy to observe the piety and modesty of the men and woman in that region. This was due to the endless efforts of the pious scholars, especially Maulānā Abdullāh Haripuri ؒ, who completely transformed the region as though it was a garden of paradise. I even saw billboards stating that un-Islamic songs and music were not allowed in this region.

Thursday 22nd December 2016

I lead the Fajr Salāh in the Masjid of Shāmpur and then spoke briefly on the virtues of Fajr Salāh quoting the verse,

$$\text{أَقِمِ الصَّلَاةَ لِدُلُوكِ الشَّمْسِ إِلَىٰ غَسَقِ اللَّيْلِ وَقُرْآنَ الْفَجْرِ إِنَّ قُرْآنَ الْفَجْرِ كَانَ مَشْهُودًا}$$

"Establish Salāh from the decline of the sun until the darkness of the night as well as the Fajr Salāh. Indeed the Fajr Salāh is attended." (17:78)

I also explained regarding our daily Ma'mūlāt (spiritual practices). Just then, the Imām announced that those mothers and sisters that wanted to spiritually link up and rectify their lives should arrive at a particular location. Subhān-Allāh, within half an hour, approximately 1000 mothers and sisters flocked into the building. After a short talk in the Bengali language about the importance of reformation, all the women folk took Bai'ah verbally.

After the event, many water vessels and oil bottles were presented to me to perform Dam (blow for blessings) which delayed our next programme. On our way, we halted at a Madrasah run by the great scholar Mufti Abdul Malik, a classmate of Maulāna Asjad Madani Sāhib. I imparted a Dars (lesson) of Sahīh al-Bukhāri and then headed for Nabigonj. Our companion in this journey, Hāji Dobir Miah Sāhib had organised a Jalsa in his Madrasah Sirājul Ulūm, for the completion of Tahfīzul-Qur'ān of eight students. I was privileged to be a part of this programme and to tie the turbans on the heads of these blessed and fortunate students.

Our next programme, was in an institute in Bahubal which was assisted financially by Hāfiz Firdous Sāhib of Luton who had invited me to pay a visit. It was a well worth visit. I had rarely observed students and staff as humble as those I observed in this visit. They held my hands and cried for me to do Du'ā for their progress to the extent that 5-6 year old children came crying that I pray for them.

From there, we visited the famous Madrasah in Bahubal which was the same Madrasah my father-in-law taught and studied. I gave a brief Dars of Bukhārī Sharīf to the students before Ishā Salāh. Our food and night stay was organised by Mufti Mash'hūd and Maulāna Mashkūr, the brothers of Maulāna Ubaidul Haque Sāhib.

Friday 23rd December 2016

In the morning, we had breakfast in the home town of my close colleague, Maulāna Ubaidul Haque Sāhib and then Bai'ah took place for all those who were repeatedly requesting for their self-rectification. From there, we halted to pray for the completion of a Masjid in the locality which was being built.

Our next important programme was in the college of Banyachong which was organised by Maulāna Abdul-Halīm Sāhib and his friends, after the success of the previous year's programme. The programme was in English and many professors and graduates of universities attended the seminar which was titled 'Mercy for Mankind.' In the seminar, I highlighted the prominent qualities of our beloved Prophet ﷺ. I explained that celebrities are followed for three reasons; Jamāl, Kamāl and Nawāl (beauty, excellence and contribution). If we ponder over these qualities, then we can come to the conclusion that the Prophet ﷺ, the paragon of Allāh ﷻ's creation, had these qualities in the highest form, hence we should follow him. The seminar concluded with a question and answer session and refreshments and gifts for all the attendees.

Jumu'ah speech and Salāh on this day was organised in Dārul Qur'ān Masjid. In the speech, I highlighted the importance and virtues of Jumu'ah and our wrong attitude towards its significance.

After Asr Salāh, we visited the institute of Mufti Mashāhid Sāhib, a scholar who resides in Makkah Mukarramah. He had diligently arranged through his elder brother, a short talk and Du'ā and he requested that I observe the progress and the construction work of the girls Madrasah. Mufti Mashāhid Sāhib had been working tirelessly, spending whatever money he could save and raise for the day to day running of the Madrasah as well as the construction work. Food and overnight stay was in Modhukhani – the residence of Maulāna Juhair Sāhib.

Saturday 24th December 2016

In the morning, we visited the famous institute of Shaykh Asghar Husain Nūri ﷺ, one of the great students and disciples of Shaykhul

Islām Maulāna Husain Ahmad Madani ﷺ. I was repeatedly requested to visit the institute by my honourable friend, Maulāna Afzal Chawdhry Sāhib in the UK – the Imām of Shāh-Jalāl Jāmi' Masjid, Leeds. I was overwhelmed by the warm reception and the recitation and Nashīds of the students.

There, we visited the grave of the late Shaykh and then set off for Banyachong for our Islāhi Majlis. This programme was arranged many months in advance with full publicity, hence a large crowd of people from the locals, including the students of Dārul Qur'ān attended. All those who took Bai'ah previously, attended the programme and it proved very beneficial for the masses, Alhamdulillāh.

In the interim, I was booked for a Tafsīr session in Banyachong for the evening due to the fact that the regular guest, the famous scholar Shaykh Nūrul Islām Sāhib Walipuri, was ill and had gone abroad for treatment. I was surprised to observe the sheer amount of people flocking in the market area for this three day event. I highlighted in my Tafsīr session the Qur'anic verses,

$$\text{وَعِبَادُ الرَّحْمَٰنِ الَّذِينَ يَمْشُونَ عَلَى الْأَرْضِ هَوْنًا وَإِذَا خَاطَبَهُمُ الْجَاهِلُونَ قَالُوا سَلَامًا}$$

"[True] servants of the Most Gracious are [only] they who walk gently on earth and who, whenever the foolish address them, they reply with [words of] peace." (25:63)

I explained how important it is for us to achieve the noble traits mentioned in the last Rukū of Sūrah Furqān such as humility, sincerity, tolerance, patience and devotion in worship. The speech was received with applause due to it being completely different from the normal themes of the other scholars.

Sunday 25th December 2016

In the morning after Fajr, I was invited for breakfast by a leading scholar who runs an institute in Banyachong. After breakfast, we headed for Nabigonj where I observed a business initiative set by my close colleague Maulāna Juhair Sāhib with his friends in an area of over 100 acres. I marvelled at the breath-taking scene which comprised of over 45 reservoirs, lakes and ponds in which they were producing fish for wholesaling. Throughout the area, there were hundreds of trees and different types of fruits and vegetables which transformed the place into a beautiful, exotic and gigantic garden. I was requested to place some tadpoles and small fishes in the ponds and then conclude with a brief speech and Du'ā about the virtues and importance of trustworthiness in business.

From there, we proceeded towards Mullachok, the residence of my cousin brother, Maulāna Abdul-Quddūs who remains my closest attendant and colleague throughout all my journeys in Bangladesh. The set programme was based on spirituality and tents were hired due to the massive turnout. After the programme, all the attendants took Bai'ah and the programme concluded with an emotional Du'ā and a delicious meal. In Mullachok, all my relatives from my mother's side turned up. Hence, I was meeting each and every one till late in the night resulting in very less sleep.

Monday 26th December 2016

In the morning, I went to visit the graves of my maternal grandparents in Akilpur, Sylhet and then had breakfast in my maternal uncle, Ayyūb Ali's residence. From there, we set off to visit my eldest maternal uncle, Arab Ali in Baluchor, in the heart of Sylhet town. Hospitality was natural in the people of Bangladesh, especially towards relatives, hence at every stop, a full meal with varieties of dishes and savouries was prepared.

From there, we visited a relative of my colleague, Hāfiz Kawthar, in one of the highest top class hotels of Sylhet. Our midday meal was fixed in Hāfiz Nūrul Ahmad's residence, who had also travelled to Bangladesh. By then, we had no space for a morsel!

Subsequently, we visited one of our close colleagues, brother Zubair, who is the brother of Maulāna Abdur Rahmān Sāhib of Makkah Mukarramah. He had been waiting anxiously throughout our entire journey for us to visit his residence. I could only have a cup of tea before resuming our journey to our next stop, Silawra Jagannatpur – the hometown of Hāfiz Kawthar.

It was a very bumpy ride and the people of the region were not welcoming in the beginning. Alhamdulillāh, after my speech in broken Bangla, they inclined towards us and requested us earnestly to stay overnight. They also promised to hold a large conference in the future. The programme was received positively, Alhamdulillāh and whilst we were returning to our place of rest in Biswanath, we were inundated with phone calls about the success of the programme in an area deprived of the correct teachings of Islām. I was very pleased with the outcome and praised Allāh ﷻ for the success. We stayed overnight in the residence of Maulāna Habīb-ur-Rahmān Sāhib, the principal of Jāmiah Muhammadiyah in Biswanath.

Tuesday 27th December 2016

In the morning after having breakfast in the residence of Maulāna Habīb-ur-Rahmān Sāhib, I went to pay a visit to my relatives in my village (Duhal). From there, we set off for Dayāmir, where we were invited by Shaykh Mashāhid Sāhib, the father of Maulāna Bilāl Sāhib (Bradford). After that, we visited the great institute, Jāmiah Islāmiyah, Gohorpur – established by the great scholar of Islām, Muhaddith-Asr, Shaykhul Islām, Maulāna Muhammad Nūrul Islām Gohorpūri ﷫.

The Shaykh's son, who is now currently running the institute very smoothly, welcomed us into his office and provided us with an up to date report of the institute. After leading the Maghrib Salāh in the Masjid of the institute, we visited the grave of the late Shaykh, who was a close student and attendant of Shaykhul Islām, Maulāna Husain Ahmad Madani ﷫. The Shaykh studied his final years in the world renowned institute Dārul Ulūm Deoband and he completed his final year by achieving first position in Bukhārī class.

Gohorpūr Madrasah

From there, we visited Jāmiah Islāmia Kazi-Bazār, a well-established institute in the heart of Sylhet district run by the great Mujāhid of Islām and Principal, Maulāna Habīb-ur Rahmān Sāhib. He had just returned from the UK and whilst in the UK, he had repeatedly requested me to visit his institute, hence, I needed to fulfil his wishes. Even though he was very ill and had previously suffered from heart attacks and strokes, he patiently waited for my arrival, missing his important programmes and engagements in the process. Alhamdulillāh, I was very impressed with the great work taking place in the institute. I also met the supervisor Mufti Shafīq, the son in law of Mufti Fārūq Barūni who is very diligently and tirelessly working for the progress of the Madrasah.

Our day ended with a visit to Satayhal Nabigonj, the village of my father-in-law where we stayed overnight.

Wednesday 28th December 2016

After Fajr Salāh, we were scheduled to have breakfast in Satayhal, in the residence of Hāfiz Abul-Layth Sāhib, a friend of mine from Dārul Ulūm Bury days. After breakfast, we set off for our main programme of the day in Manikgonj, a Madrasah established by one of our colleagues with the same name as me, Mufti Saiful Islām Sāhib. After reaching there, I spoke first to the students of the girls' Madrasah and then the boys' Madrasah. I was very impressed to observe the immense progress within a very short amount of time. Mufti Sāhib—an energetic young and active scholar, had been requesting me to come over for the opening for the last few years but I could not pen it into my tight schedule. Alhamdulillāh, it was a worthwhile visit in which he kindly requested me to become the patron of the institute.

From there, we had supper which was scheduled at our colleague, brother Fayrūz's house. On the way back, there was a traffic jam which delayed all our programmes. After a quick meal at brother Fayrūz's house and performing the Tahnīk (blessing) on his newborn child, we headed for Madrasah Qāsim-ul-Ulūm for a long needed rest. By then, it was already past 1:00am.

Thursday 29th December 2016

After Fajr Salāh, we headed for the institute which was named after our beloved teacher, Shaykul Hadīth, Maulāna Bilāl Sāhib. The principal of the institute, Shaykh Sa'di was so persistent in taking me there despite my reluctancy due to my lack of sleep and seeing all my travel colleagues in a very lethargic condition. He was not taking no for an answer and had already arrived with his latest model car to take us to his institute. He reminded me that I had to bless his Madrasah every time I stepped my foot in Bangladesh. This was all due to his immense affection for this humble servant.

I addressed the gathering, in which there were also mothers and sisters from all the adjacent villages, in Bangla. After speaking to the students, I briefly touched on the topic of Salāh and Hijāb for our sisters. I mentioned to the sisters that Allāh ﷻ has prescribed 3 pieces of cloth as the Kafn (shroud) for the male, whilst 5 pieces are prescribed for the female. This is because they need to be concealed properly. The two extra cloths are for the upper part of the body - the Sīnaband which is a cloth for covering the chest and the Ornī which is a cloth for covering the head. These parts of the female anatomy are very seductive and alluring for the normal male, thus they require extra covering. It is as though Allāh ﷻ is addressing the females saying, "O' my female servants, you cannot return back to Me in a shameless and immodest state like the way you lived in this world; when you come to Me, you need to be well-dressed." Allāhu Akbar!

Subsequently, we set off for our main programme for which I was the chief guest, held at Markazul Hudā, Signboard, Demra. We had a large and noisy reception by the students standing on both sides of the road welcoming us, loudly chanting "Ahlan Wa Sahlan Wa-Marhaban – welcome and greetings." My talk was scheduled for 8pm after Ishā and I was requested to speak for at least 2 hours. I spoke on the importance of change, keeping the beautiful verse as the main focus,

$$\text{أَلَمْ يَأْنِ لِلَّذِينَ آمَنُوا أَن تَخْشَعَ قُلُوبُهُمْ لِذِكْرِ اللَّهِ وَمَا نَزَلَ مِنَ الْحَقِّ}$$

"Has the time not come for the hearts of the believers to submit to Allāh's remembrance and to the truth that has been revealed?" (57:16)

I spoke in length and detail about bringing a change and quoted the great scholar and saint Fudhayl Ibn Iyādh ﷺ, who in the beginning of his life was a burglar and a dacoit, but Subhān-Allāh when Allāh ﷻ wants to change anyone, He provides the means. Hence, once, Fudhayl Ibn Iyādh ﷺ was heading towards meeting his mistress at night when he entered a house in which the occupant was reciting the Holy Qur'ān in his Tahajjud Salāh. What a coincidence! He recited the above verse and when Shaykh Fudhayl heard the verse, he immediately kneeled down and cried out.

$$\text{بَلَى يَا رَبِّي قَدْ آنَ وَقَدْ حَانَ}$$

"Why not my Lord? The time is here and the time is now."

I reminded myself and all the thousands of people who were now fully focused to respond to the call in a positive way like Shaykh Fudhayl Ibn Iyādh ﷺ did and to repent and reform. Everyone pronounced after me, "Balā Yā Rabbi, Qad Āna Wa Qad Hāna" and they became emotional with their eyes tearing. May Allāh ﷻ make this programme a means of rectification and reformation, Āmīn.

During this programme, I met many eminent scholars and pious elders. At the end of my day's programme, I visited Madrasah Ibrāhīmiyah due to a heartfelt request from the principal, Mufti Shafīq Sāhib – a senior disciple of Mufti Mahmūd Hasan Gongohi ﷺ. When I passed by the Bukhāri class students, they immediately gathered together requesting me to advise them. Students from all the different classes and boarding rooms started getting out of their beds and joined in the programme which concluded with a brief Du'ā.

Friday 30th December 2016

After Fajr Salāh, I was informed that our well renowned scholar, and general secretary of Khatme-Nubuwwat, Bangladesh, Shaykh Nūrul-Islām Sāhib lived next to our place of stay that night– the home of Maulāna Abdul Halīm Sāhib. I was overjoyed and immediately made arrangements to visit him. He was brimming with happiness and joy when he met me and my colleague Maulāna Abdus-Salām Sāhib. We had a refreshing breakfast and a lengthy conversation on many different issues. He showed us around the beautiful Masjid and Madrasah which he had established near his residence. This is apart from the big institute that he runs in Kilgaw, Dhaka which was located half an hour drive from where he lived.

After bidding farewell, we headed off for another great scholar's residence and Madrasah, Shaykh Āshiqur-Rahmān Sāhib in Sabar, two hours drive from our place of residence. We just managed to reach there in time for Jumu'ah Salāh which I was requested to lead by our host.

After food and rest, our host announced that I will be laying the foundation for the big reservoir for the water supply of the institute. Hence, we headed for the fields. I and other colleagues dug the initial ground and we were privileged to lay the foundation brick for the wall of the big tank and reservoir. Shaykh Āshiqur-Rahmān Sāhib showed us around his gigantic Madrasah area consisting of over 12 acres. He had all types of fruit trees and even the different types of date palms, including Ajwa, Mabrūm and Safāwi. He narrated that he had spent over 30 lacs (£30,000) just on plants, seeds and fertilisers for his plantation fields. I marvelled at the beautiful and breath taking scenes and wished I could stay longer, but we had to move on.

Next, Maulāna Ahmad Madani had organised a programme in Baridara Madrasah, Dhaka – a great institute of learning which is run by the well renowned Islamic scholar, Shaykh Nūr Husain Qāsimi.

We halted there for a while and after Ishā, I addressed the students about their duties and responsibilities and the importance of valuing their student days. I put forward three points, which were,

1. To correct our intention for our pursuance of this sacred knowledge,
2. Practicing upon what we learn,
3. And strict adherence to the Sunnah.

We were also fortunate to meet and benefit from the company of the great scholar of the institute and of Bangladesh, Shaykh Ubaidullāh Fārūq Sāhib. He also presented me with his remarkable book written in Arabic– Āthārul Hadīth. They insisted us to eat, but we were already fixed for food and overnight stay in Maulāna Abdul Halīm's house.

Saturday 31st December 2016

After performing Fajr Salāh, I went back to sleep due to being exhausted and stressed out from the ever increasing programmes. After Zuhr Salāh, we set off for Chittagong which was originally scheduled for after Fajr, but due to the three days of Ijtimā of Tablīgh Jamā'at being held in Chittagong, near Hathazari Madrasah and at the same time in Sylhet, it was delayed. It was estimated that in each of the Ijtimās, up to 1.5 million people attended. May Allāh ﷻ make these gatherings a means of goodness, wakefulness and activeness in the Muslim Ummah at a time when it is going through so much persecution and oppression. Āmīn!

A Land of Natural Beauty

Alhamdulillāh, it was a sound decision to delay our journey to Chittagong because even after reaching our first destination, Mazāhirul Ulūm, Chitagong, students, staff and other people were still stuck in the traffic and were waiting for the availability of transport. The present Principal, Maulāna Luqmān Sāhib was waiting eagerly for our arrival. He had been inviting me for the last decade to visit his institute, but due to my busy schedule and it being a long distance journey, I always put it off for later. How long could I postpone these sincere requests? Eventually, by the grace of Allāh ﷻ, He brought me to the great institute of learning.

Maulāna Luqmān Sāhib showed me around the whole building and explained to me the progress of the Madrasah in the last decade. The progress of the Madrasah was evident from the students work and the expansion of the Madrasah's building and classrooms. May Allāh ﷻ accept his efforts and give him full recovery from the heart operation which he underwent. Even though, he was physically weak, he actively walked around everywhere. We concluded our day with a supper consisting of a wide range of dishes.

It was 12 midnight when we began to hear fireworks from all corners of the Madrasah. It saddened me to hear and learn that despite being Muslims, we have forgotten our own rituals and obligations and have began to follow the rituals of other religions. Surprisingly, even in the UK, I do not normally hear this many fireworks being used.

The point for us to consider is that Allāh ﷻ has given us a beautiful religion which is a complete code of life. There is nothing left that we have not been informed about. From morning to dusk and from birth till death, everything has been explained in details in our wonderful religion, Islām. It is us that have forsaken the true faith and have started to emulate other faiths and religions.

This reminded me of a scholar who once stood upon the Mimbar and said, "I have some good news and bad news for you. The good news is that we have enough money to build a Masjid, but the bad news is that the money is still in our pockets." In exactly the same way, we have the solution for the problems in the world and we have a perfect code of life, but we are not practicing upon it. Other faiths and religions have taken our social etiquettes and morals and surpassed us in the worldly life. May Allāh ﷻ give us the true understanding of the Dīn and may He give us the Tawfīq (ability) to follow it in its entirety. Āmīn!

Sunday 1st January 2017

After performing Fajr Salāh, the students carried out their Ma'mūlāt of Tasbīh-Fātimi, Durūd Sharīf and Sūrah Yāsīn, concluding with a Du'ā. One of the senior teachers stood up after the Du'ā and announced that I would be speaking to the staff and students. I addressed the audience in Urdu, highlighting the virtues of knowledge and that the students needed to value their days of studying. I concluded the programme with a supplication.

After breakfast, which was more like a heavy dinner, we set off for the largest institute in Bangladesh, Muīnul Islām Hathazari, which accommodated over 8,000 students. We were privileged to meet all the senior scholars of the institute, especially Shaykh Junaid Baburnogori and Shaykhul Islām Maulāna Ahmad Shafī Sāhib and Mufti Abdus-Salām Chātgami. Shaykh Junaid Baburnogori was the son of the great scholar, Shaykh Abul Hasan Chātgami ﷺ - the author of 'Tanzīmul-Ashtāt-li-Halli-Awīsātil-Miskhkāt', a unique commentary on the famous Hadīth book, Mishkātul Masābīh. It is a unique commentary which makes one independent from many other commentaries - an entire ocean in a pot. Even till today, I study and recommend this commentary to my students and friends. Shaykh gifted us with his written books and showed great hospitality.

Mufti Abdus-Salām Chātgami is a high profile, brilliant, experienced Mufti. He is the author of many books and the student of Mufti Shafī Sāhib ﷺ, Maulāna Yūsuf Binnori ﷺ and many other distinguished scholars. He was the grand Mufti of Binnori Town after Mufti Wali Hasan Sāhib ﷺ but due to ill health, he had to return back to Bangladesh. He spoke to me and my colleagues and gifted us with many of his compilations and books.

Allāmah Ahmad Shafī Sāhib, the chief principal and Shaykhul-Hadīth of the institute graced us with his Ziyārat (visit). Māshā-Allāh, he is aged over 93 and one of the last remaining disciples of Shaykul Islām, Maulāna Husain Ahmad Madani ﷺ. He gave us a warm reception with his words of spirituality and then supplicated for all of us, with his sincere and accepted Du'ās. We performed our Zuhr Salāh in his chamber and then had our lunch in the guest room with him.

Our organiser in Hathazari, Maulāna Muīnud-Dīn, the special attendant of Allāmah Ahmad Shafī Sāhib, who I have met on several occasions in the UK, requested me, alongside Maulāna Luqmān Sāhib, to address the final year students with some advice. I was humbled by their request and initially wanted to decline, but they prompted me to speak.

It was a breath taking atmosphere of spirituality and tranquillity in the Dārul Hadīth – a large hall which accommodated 2,700 students all studying their final year of Ālim class. It was by far, the largest Dawra-Hadīth (final Hadīth year) class in Bangladesh, if not in the world. I addressed them briefly, conscious of the fact that Mufti Kifāyatulāh Sāhib, the Tirmizi Sharīf teacher, spared his own time to accommodate my speech. I briefly touched upon the 4 qualities that each and every student should inculcate and possess before they graduate from this magnificent institute of learning. These qualities have been mentioned by Hasan Al-Basri ﷺ, quoted by Mulla Ali Qāri ﷺ in Mirqāt – the commentary of Mishkāt. He states,

$$\text{إِنَّمَا الْفَقِيهُ الزَّاهِدُ فِي الدُّنْيَا، الرَّاغِبُ الَى الْآخِرَةِ، الْبَصِيرُ بِأَمْرِ دِينِهِ الْمُدَاوِمُ عَلَى عِبَادَةِ رَبِّهِ}$$

"Indeed a true scholar (jurist) is the one who is abstinent in the

Dunya, desirous for the Ākhirah, has insight (knowledge) in the matters of Dīn and is punctual in the worship of his Lord."

Each and every student listened with complete focus and dedication which was apparent from their sitting postures and facial expressions.

After the brief talk, I thanked Mufti Kifāyatullāh Sāhib for giving me this opportunity and he also thanked me for giving his students the opportunity to benefit. I thanked and expressed my gratitude to Allāh ﷻ for affording me this great moment in my life, Alhamdulillāh.

Our next destination was Patya Madrasah which is also situated in Chittagong. The last time I visited these two institutes was 10 years ago in 2007 on our way to Cox Bazār. I was looking forward to meeting our host of 2007, Maulāna Abū Tāhir Nadwi Sāhib, who on several occasions had visited the UK. We eventually reached Patya at the time when the congregation of Asr Salāh was taking place. I was amazed at the incredible fact that I barely noticed a single student wondering around at the time of Salāh despite there being over 5,000 students in the Madrasah. We quickly performed our Wudhū and performed our own congregation in the guest room.

After Salāh, we met the principal of the institute, Shaykh Abdul Halīm Bukhārī, who was very kind and humble in nature. He instructed Shaykh Abū Tāhir Nadwi for my speech to be addressed in the Madrasah and for him to cater for our hospitality well. After Maghrib Salāh, I spoke in detail regarding the four qualities which I spoke briefly about in Hathazari Madrasah. I elaborated on each point with Qur'anic verses, Ahādīth, sayings of pious predecessors and parables. I concluded the speech with a Du'ā which became very emotional. The entire Masjid was echoing with the sobbing and crying of the students. After the Du'ā, it became difficult to leave the Masjid without shaking hands with the 5,000 students. They raced towards me and the staff and my colleagues had to control the crowd. I reassured them that I would not leave until I had met everyone and Alhamdulillāh, I managed to fulfil this. May Allāh ﷻ make this a means for my salvation in this world and the Hereafter. Āmīn!

After this programme, our initial decision was to head back to Dhaka, however, after brief consultation, we decided to stay overnight due to the busy traffic at night from Chittagong to Dhaka. After having supper in the guest room, we went for a walk outside the Madrasah which took away our stress of the day. Throughout our journey, at every programme, many scholars, principals, Imāms and well-wishers strongly requested for programmes in their respected institutes and Masjids, which I had to politely decline due to the lack of time and the oversubscribed and overwhelming programmes. We slept very late due the great amount of visitors, scholars and students meeting us.

Monday 2nd January 2017

All our colleagues woke up at the beginning time of Fajr and after performing our Fajr Salāh in Jamā'at, we set off for Dhaka at 5:30am. After a few hours, we halted at Nūr Jahān service station for tea and breakfast and then headed straight to the residence of Maulāna Abdul Halīm Nu'māni, where our lunch was scheduled.

Before lunch, I and few of my colleagues headed for the market place to purchase a few items to bring back as gifts for our families and friends. Due to the number of overwhelming programmes, I virtually had no time to even step into any shop during the entire journey. Alhamdulillāh, within an hour, we purchased a few items and then returned back to our resting place.

On the way, the son of Shaykh Nūrul Islām Sāhib, Maulāna Khālid met us and requested us to pay a visit to their residence. Hence, a few of my colleagues and I went to meet Shaykh Nūrul Islām Sāhib, who was waiting in anticipation for us outside his home. He gave us a warm reception and we had tea and snacks together. Thereafter, I lead Maghrib Salāh in his residence. At the time of departure, he gifted me with a Lungi and Abā (cloak), which I really cherished due to it being from a very highly reputable scholar.

Our next destination was the home of my close friend and companion, Maulāna Sharīf-ud-Dīn Sāhib. He left us in advance to make full preparations for our supper and overnight stay. Māshā-Allāh, he did more than that which was expected and our last night's stay became a memorable night to remember for the future. Friends and colleagues continuously came to visit us including a very close friend, Fayrūz who brought along his father. I was overwhelmed with emotion to see his elderly father who was clearly disabled physically but out of love, had came to see me. He and his son gave me some gifts and cried profusely at the time of departure.

My colleagues and companions of Bangladesh continued to engage with emotional conversation and pleaded for forgiveness for all their shortcomings. I became emotional and requested them to forgive me for my shortcomings throughout the journey and thanked them whole-heartedly for leaving all their important commitments to accompany me from the beginning of the journey to the end. May Allāh ﷻ reward them immensely for their affection, love and sacrifice. Āmīn.

Tuesday 3rd January 2017

I only had a couple of hours of sleep, waking up at about 4:30am. I woke the rest of my colleagues and we performed our Fajr Salāh in Jamā'at at 5:30 am. We then set off for the airport. On the way, my colleague, Maulānā Ahmad Madani informed me, after checking our flight details for the Saudi airlines flight SV803, heading for Jeddah had been delayed by 4 hours. Nonetheless, we proceeded towards Hazrat Shāh Jalāl International Airport, reaching there at 7:00 am. After checking our luggage and receiving our boarding passes, we exited the airport for a few hours having taken permission from the authorities.

At this point, Maulāna Sufyān Ahmad, the founder and principal of Talīmul-Qur'ān Madrasah strongly requested us to visit his institute, which was located on College Road, Biman Bandar, Dhaka, very close to the airport. Hence, we decided to visit his institute and meet his staff and students. After having a refreshing breakfast, we took an hour's nap and then headed back for the airport. Due to already having checked in, we proceeded towards the immigration and set off for Jeddah at 2:05pm for a flight lasting over 7 hours.

Alhamdulillāh, we landed in Jeddah at King Abdul Azīz International Airport at 6:20pm. We had approximately 7 hours before the transit flight to Manchester, so I decided to jot down briefly our memorable journey of Bangladesh. May Allāh ﷻ accept this humble effort and make it a means for the salvation of myself and all those who benefit in any way from these few pages. Āmīn.

Other titles from JKN Publications

Your Questions Answered
An outstanding book written by Shaykh Mufti Saiful Islām. A very comprehensive yet simple Fatāwa book and a source of guidance that reaches out to a wider audience i.e. the English speaking Muslims. The reader will benefit from the various answers to questions based on the Laws of Islām relating to the beliefs of Islām, knowledge, Sunnah, pillars of Islām, marriage, divorce and contemporary issues.

UK RRP: £7.50

Hadeeth for Beginners
A concise Hadeeth book with various Ahādeeth that relate to basic Ibādāh and moral etiquettes in Islām accessible to a wider readership. Each Hadeeth has been presented with the Arabic text, its translation and commentary to enlighten the reader, its meaning and application in day-to-day life.

UK RRP: £3.00

Du'ā for Beginners
This book contains basic Du'ās which every Muslim should recite on a daily basis. Highly recommended to young children and adults studying at Islamic schools and Madrasahs so that one may cherish the beautiful treasure of supplications of our beloved Prophet ﷺ in one's daily life, which will ultimately bring peace and happiness in both worlds, Inshā-Allāh.

UK RRP: £2.00

How well do you know Islām?
An exciting educational book which contains 300 multiple questions and answers to help you increase your knowledge on Islām! Ideal for the whole family, especially children and adult students to learn new knowledge in an enjoyable way and cherish the treasures of knowledge that you will acquire from this book. A very beneficial tool for educational syllabus.

UK RRP: £3.00

Treasures of the Holy Qur'ān
This book entitled "Treasures of the Holy Qur'ān" has been compiled to create a stronger bond between the Holy Qur'ān and the readers. It mentions the different virtues of Sūrahs and verses from the Holy Qur'ān with the hope that the readers will increase their zeal and enthusiasm to recite and inculcate the teachings of the Holy Qur'ān into their daily lives.

UK RRP: £3.00

Marriage - A Complete Solution

Islām regards marriage as a great act of worship. This book has been designed to provide the fundamental teachings and guidelines of all what relates to the marital life in a simplified English language. It encapsulates in a nutshell all the marriage laws mentioned in many of the main reference books in order to facilitate their understanding and implementation.

UK RRP: £5.00

Pearls of Luqmān

This book is a comprehensive commentary of Sūrah Luqmān, written beautifully by Shaykh Mufti Saiful Islām. It offers the reader with an enquiring mind, abundance of advice, guidance, counselling and wisdom.

The reader will be enlightened by many wonderful topics and anecdotes mentioned in this book, which will create a greater understanding of the Holy Qur'ān and its wisdom. The book highlights some of the wise sayings and words of advice Luqmān ؑ gave to his son.

UK RRP: £3.00

Arabic Grammar for Beginners

This book is a study of Arabic Grammar based on the subject of Nahw (Syntax) in a simplified English format. If a student studies this book thoroughly, he/she will develop a very good foundation in this field, Inshā-Allāh. Many books have been written on this subject in various languages such as Arabic, Persian and Urdu. However, in this day and age there is a growing demand for this subject to be available in English.

UK RRP: £3.00

A Gift to My Youngsters

This treasure filled book, is a collection of Islamic stories, morals and anecdotes from the life of our beloved Prophet ﷺ, his Companions ؓ and the pious predecessors. The stories and anecdotes are based on moral and ethical values, which the reader will enjoy sharing with their peers, friends, families and loved ones.

"A Gift to My Youngsters" – is a wonderful gift presented to the readers personally, by the author himself, especially with the youngsters in mind. He has carefully selected stories and anecdotes containing beautiful morals, lessons and valuable knowledge and wisdom.

UK RRP: £5.00

Travel Companion

The beauty of this book is that it enables a person on any journey, small or distant or simply at home, to utilise their spare time to read and benefit from an exciting and vast collection of important and interesting Islamic topics and lessons. Written in simple and easy to read text, this book will immensely benefit both the newly interested person in Islām and the inquiring mind of a student expanding upon their existing knowledge. Inspiring reminders from the Holy Qur'ān and the blessed words of our beloved Prophet ﷺ beautifies each topic and will illuminate the heart of the reader.   **UK RRP: £5.00**

Pearls of Wisdom

Junaid Baghdādī ؓ once said, "Allāh ﷻ strengthens through these Islamic stories the hearts of His friends, as proven from the Qur'anic verse,
"And all that We narrate unto you of the stories of the Messengers, so as to strengthen through it your heart." (11:120)
Mālik Ibn Dinār ؓ stated that such stories are gifts from Paradise. He also emphasised to narrate these stories as much as possible as they are gems and it is possible that an individual might find a truly rare and invaluable gem among them.   **UK RRP: £6.00**

Inspirations

This book contains a compilation of selected speeches delivered by Shaykh Mufti Saiful Islām on a variety of topics such as the Holy Qur'ān, Nikāh and eating Halāl. Having previously been compiled in separate booklets, it was decided that the transcripts be gathered together in one book for the benefit of the reader. In addition to this, we have included in this book, further speeches which have not yet been printed.

UK RRP: £6.00

Gift to my Sisters

A thought provoking compilation of very interesting articles including real life stories of pious predecessors, imaginative illustrations and much more. All designed to influence and motivate mothers, sisters, wives and daughters towards an ideal Islamic lifestyle. A lifestyle referred to by our Creator, Allāh ﷻ in the Holy Qur'ān as the means to salvation and ultimate success.

UK RRP: £6.00

Gift to my Brothers

A thought provoking compilation of very interesting articles including real life stories of pious predecessors, imaginative illustrations, medical advices on intoxicants and rehabilitation and much more. All designed to influence and motivate fathers, brothers, husbands and sons towards an ideal Islamic lifestyle. A lifestyle referred to by our Creator, Allāh ﷻ in the Holy Qur'ān as the means to salvation and ultimate success.

UK RRP: £5.00

Heroes of Islām

"In the narratives there is certainly a lesson for people of intelligence (understanding)." (12:111)

A fine blend of Islamic personalities who have been recognised for leaving a lasting mark in the hearts and minds of people.

A distinguishing feature of this book is that the author has selected not only some of the most world and historically famous renowned scholars but also these lesser known and a few who have simply left behind a valuable piece of advice to their nearest and dearest.

UK RRP: £5.00

Ask a Mufti (3 volumes)

Muslims in every generation have confronted different kinds of challenges. Inspite of that, Islām produced such luminary Ulamā who confronted and responded to the challenges of their time to guide the Ummah to the straight path.

"Ask A Mufti" is a comprehensive three volume fatwa book, based on the Hanafi School, covering a wide range of topics related to every aspect of human life such as belief, ritual worship, life after death and contemporary legal topics related to purity, commercial transaction, marriage, divorce, food, cosmetic, laws pertaining to women, Islamic medical ethics and much more.

UK RRP: £30.00

Should I Follow a Madhab?

Taqleed or following one of the four legal schools is not a new phenomenon. Historically, scholars of great calibre and luminaries, each one being a specialist in his own right, were known to have adhered to one of the four legal schools. It is only in the previous century that a minority group emerged advocating a severe ban on following one of the four major schools.

This book endeavours to address the topic of Taqleed and elucidates its importance and necessity in this day and age. It will also, by the Divine Will of Allāh ﷻ dispel some of the confusion surrounding this topic.

UK RRP: £5.00

Advice for the Students of Knowledge

Allāh ﷻ describes divine knowledge in the Holy Qur'ān as a 'Light'. Amongst the qualities of light are purity and guidance. The Holy Prophet ﷺ has clearly explained this concept in many blessed Ahādeeth and has also taught us many supplications in which we ask for beneficial knowledge.

This book is a golden tool for every sincere student of knowledge wishing to mould his/her character and engrain those correct qualities in order to be worthy of receiving the great gift of Ilm from Allāh ﷻ.

UK RRP: £3.00

Stories for Children

"Stories for Children" - is a wonderful gift presented to the readers personally by the author himself, especially with the young children in mind. The stories are based on moral and ethical values, which the reader will enjoy sharing with their peers, friends, families and loved ones. The aim is to present to the children stories and incidents which contain moral lessons, in order to reform and correct their lives, according to the Holy Qur'ān and Sunnah.

UK RRP: £5.00

Pearls from My Shaykh
This book contains a collection of pearls and inspirational accounts of the Holy Prophet ﷺ, his noble Companions, pious predecessors and some personal accounts and sayings of our well-known contemporary scholar and spiritual guide, Shaykh Mufti Saiful Islām Sāhib. Each anecdote and narrative of the pious predecessors have been written in the way that was narrated by Mufti Saiful Islām Sāhib in his discourses, drawing the specific lessons he intended from telling the story. The accounts from the life of the Shaykh has been compiled by a particular student based on their own experience and personal observation. **UK RRP: £5.00**

Paradise & Hell
This book is a collection of detailed explanation of Paradise and Hell including the state and conditions of its inhabitants. All the details have been taken from various reliable sources. The purpose of its compilation is for the reader to contemplate and appreciate the innumerable favours, rewards, comfort and unlimited luxuries of Paradise and at the same time take heed from the punishment of Hell. Shaykh Mufti Saiful Islām Sāhib has presented this book in a unique format by including the Tafseer and virtues of Sūrah Ar-Rahmān. **UK RRP: £5.00**

Prayers for Forgiveness
Prayers for Forgiveness' is a short compilation of Du'ās in Arabic with English translation and transliteration. This book can be studied after 'Du'ā for Beginners' or as a separate book. It includes twenty more Du'ās which have not been mentioned in the previous Du'ā book. It also includes a section of Du'ās from the Holy Qur'ān and a section from the Ahādeeth. The book concludes with a section mentioning the Ninety-Nine Names of Allāh ﷻ with its translation and transliteration. **UK RRP: £3.00**

Scattered Pearls
This book is a collection of scattered pearls taken from books, magazines, emails and WhatsApp messages. These pearls will hopefully increase our knowledge, wisdom and make us realise the purpose of life. In this book, Mufti Sāhib has included messages sent to him from scholars, friends and colleagues which will be beneficial and interesting for our readers Inshā-Allāh. **UK RRP: £4.00**

Poems of Wisdom
This book is a collection of poems from those who contributed to the Al-Mumin Magazine in the poems section. The Hadeeth mentions "Indeed some form of poems are full of wisdom." The themes of each poem vary between wittiness, thought provocation, moral lessons, emotional to name but a few. The readers will benefit from this immensely and make them ponder over the outlook of life in general.
UK RRP: £4.00

Horrors of Judgement Day
This book is a detailed and informative commentary of the first three Sūrahs of the last Juz namely; Sūrah Naba, Sūrah Nāzi'āt and Sūrah Abasa. These Sūrahs vividly depict the horrific events and scenes of the Great Day in order to warn mankind the end of this world. These Sūrahs are an essential reminder for us all to instil the fear and concern of the Day of Judgement and to detach ourselves from the worldly pleasures. Reading this book allows us to attain the true realization of this world and provides essential advices of how to gain eternal salvation in the Hereafter.

RRP: £5:00

Spiritual Heart
It is necessary that Muslims always strive to better themselves at all times and to free themselves from the destructive maladies. This book focusses on three main spiritual maladies; pride, anger and evil gazes. It explains its root causes and offers some spiritual cures. Many examples from the lives of the pious predecessors are used for inspiration and encouragement for controlling the above three maladies. It is hoped that the purification process of the heart becomes easy once the underlying roots of the above maladies are clearly understood. **UK RRP: £5:00**

Hajj & Umrah for Beginners
This book is a step by step guide on Hajj and Umrah for absolute beginners. Many other additional important rulings (Masāil) have been included that will Insha-Allāh prove very useful for our readers. The book also includes some etiquettes of visiting (Ziyārat) of the Holy Prophet's ﷺ blessed Masjid and his Holy Grave.

UK RRP £3:00

Advice for the Spiritual Travellers
This book contains essential guidelines for a spiritual Murīd to gain some familiarity with the science of Tasawwuf. It explains the meaning and aims of Tasawwuf, some understanding around the concept of the soul, and general guidelines for a spiritual Murīd. This is highly recommended book and it is hoped that it gains wider readership among those Murīds who are basically new to the science of Tasawwuf.

UK RRP £3:00

Don't Worry Be Happy
This book is a compilation of sayings and earnest pieces of advice that have been gathered directly from my respected teacher Shaykh Mufti Saiful Islām Sāhib. The book consists of many valuable enlightenments including how to deal with challenges of life, promoting unity, practicing good manners, being optimistic and many other valuable advices. Our respected Shaykh has gathered this Naseehah from meditating, contemplating, analysing and searching for the gems within Qur'anic verses, Ahādeeth and teachings of our Pious Predecessors. **UK RRP £1:00**

Kanzul Bāri

Kanzul Bāri provides a detailed commentary of the Ahādeeth contained in Saheeh al-Bukhāri. The commentary includes Imām Bukhāri's ﷺ biography, the status of his book, spiritual advice, inspirational accounts along with academic discussions related to Fiqh, its application and differences of opinion. Moreover, it answers objections arising in one's mind about certain Ahādeeth. Inquisitive students of Hadeeth will find this commentary a very useful reference book in the final year of their Ālim course for gaining a deeper understanding of the science of Hadeeth. **UK RRP: £15.00**

How to Become a Friend of Allāh ﷻ

The friends of Allāh ﷻ have been described in detail in the Holy Qur'ān and Āhadeeth. This book endeavours its readers to help create a bond with Allāh ﷻ in attaining His friendship as He is the sole Creator of all material and immaterial things. It is only through Allāh's ﷻ friendship, an individual will achieve happiness in this life and the Hereafter, hence eliminate worries, sadness, depression, anxiety and misery of this world. **UK RRP: £3.00**

Gems & Jewels

This book contains a selection of articles which have been gathered for the benefit of the readers covering a variety of topics on various aspects of daily life. It offers precious advice and anecdotes that contain moral lessons. The advice captivates its readers and will extend the narrowness of their thoughts to deep reflection, wisdom and appreciation of the purpose of our existence. **UK RRP: £4.00**

End of Time

This book is a comprehensive explanation of the three Sūrahs of Juzz Amma; Sūrah Takweer, Sūrah Infitār and Sūrah Mutaffifeen. This book is a continuation from the previous book of the same author, 'Horrors of Judgement Day'. The three Sūrahs vividly sketch out the scene of the Day of Judgement and describe the state of both the inmates of Jannah and Jahannam. Mufti Saiful Islām Sāhib provides an easy but comprehensive commentary of the three Sūrahs facilitating its understanding for the readers whilst capturing the horrific scene of the ending of the world and the conditions of mankind on that horrific Day. **UK RRP: £5.00**

Andalus (modern day Spain), the long lost history, was once a country that produced many great calibre of Muslim scholars comprising of Mufassirūn, Muhaddithūn, Fuqahā, judges, scientists, philosophers, surgeons, to name but a few. The Muslims conquered Andalus in 711 AD and ruled over it for eight-hundred years. This was known as the era of Muslim glory. Many non-Muslim Europeans during that time travelled to Spain to study under Muslim scholars. The remanences of the Muslim rule in Spain are manifested through their universities, magnificent palaces and Masājid carved with Arabic writings, standing even until today. In this book, Shaykh Mufti Saiful Islām shares some of his valuable experiences he witnessed during his journey to Spain. **UK RRP: £3.00**

Ideal Youth
This book contains articles gathered from various social media avenues; magazines, emails, WhatsApp and telegram messages that provide useful tips of advice for those who have the zeal to learn and consider changing their negative habits and behavior and become better Muslims to set a positive trend for the next generation. **UK RRP:£4:00**

Ideal Teacher
This book contains abundance of precious advices for the Ulamā who are in the teaching profession. It serves to present Islamic ethical principles of teaching and to remind every teacher of their moral duties towards their students. This book will Inshā-Allāh prove to be beneficial for newly graduates and scholars wanting to utilize their knowledge through teaching. **UK RRP:£4:00**

Ideal Student
This book is a guide for all students of knowledge in achieving the excellent qualities of becoming an ideal student. It contains precious advices, anecdotes of our pious predecessors and tips in developing good morals as a student. Good morals is vital for seeking knowledge. A must for all students if they want to develop their Islamic Knowledge. **UK RRP:£4:00**

Ideal Parents
This book contains a wealth of knowledge in achieving the qualities of becoming ideal parents. It contains precious advices, anecdotes of our pious predecessors and tips in developing good parenthood skills. Good morals is vital for seeking knowledge. A must for all parents . **UK RRP:£4:00**

Ideal Couple
This book is a compilation of inspiring stories and articles containing useful tips and life skills for every couple. Marriage life is a big responsibility and success in marriage is only possible if the couple know what it means to be an ideal couple. **UK RRP:£4:00**

Ideal Role Model
This book is a compilation of sayings and accounts of our pious predecessors. The purpose of this book is so we can learn from our pious predecessors the purpose of this life and how to attain closer to the Creator. Those people who inspires us attaining closeness to our Creator are our true role models. A must everyone to read. **UK RRP:£4:00**